Redefining Cross-Border Financial Flows

Transforming Remittances with AI and Other Technologies

Hari Prasad Josyula

Apress®

Redefining Cross-Border Financial Flows: Transforming Remittances with AI and Other Technologies

Hari Prasad Josyula
Princeton, NJ, USA

ISBN-13 (pbk): 979-8-8688-1063-3 ISBN-13 (electronic): 979-8-8688-1064-0
https://doi.org/10.1007/979-8-8688-1064-0

Managing Director, Apress Media LLC: Welmoed Spahr
Acquisitions Editor: Shivangi Ramachandran
Development Editor: James Markham
Coordinating Editor: Gryffin Winkler

Cover image designed by eStudioCalamar

Distributed to the book trade worldwide by Springer Science+Business Media New York, 233 Spring Street, 6th Floor, New York, NY 10013. Phone 1-800-SPRINGER, fax (201) 348-4505, e-mail orders-ny@springer-sbm.com, or visit www.springeronline.com. Apress Media, LLC is a California LLC and the sole member (owner) is Springer Science + Business Media Finance Inc (SSBM Finance Inc). SSBM Finance Inc is a **Delaware** corporation.

For information on translations, please e-mail booktranslations@springernature.com; for reprint, paperback, or audio rights, please e-mail bookpermissions@springernature.com.

Apress titles may be purchased in bulk for academic, corporate, or promotional use. eBook versions and licenses are also available for most titles. For more information, reference our Print and eBook Bulk Sales web page at http://www.apress.com/bulk-sales.

Any source code or other supplementary material referenced by the author in this book can be found here: https://www.apress.com/gp/services/source-code.

If disposing of this product, please recycle the paper

Table of Contents

About the Author

Hari Prasad Josyula is a fintech product transformation expert with over 15 years' experience in delivering innovative customer-centric solutions. He is currently a product analyst at Dow Jones. He is a functional solution architect across banking, asset and wealth management, financial services, regulatory compliance and reporting, logistics and supply chains. He is also a certified scrum product owner, ITIL service manager and scrum master with a strong background in data analytics, business analysis and agile methodologies.

His research interests include artificial intelligence (AI) in banking (anti-money laundering, fraud and risk management), generative AI for operational efficiency in financial services, open banking, blockchain and cryptocurrencies, central bank digital currencies, embedded payments, programmable payments, financial risk management, and product, programme and portfolio management.

Josyula has an MBA in Finance from Suffolk University, Boston, MA, and an MS in Physical Sciences from Andhra University, India.

www.linkedin.com/in/harij/

scholar.google.com/citations?user=n88bVlgAAAAJ&hl=en

www.researchgate.net/profile/Hari-Prasad-Josyula

Preface

The global remittance sector and artificial intelligence (AI) work together in a way that is testament to the revolutionary force of innovation in the always changing financial and technology landscape. The book *Redefining Cross-Border Financial Flows: Transforming Remittances with AI and Other Technologies* takes readers on a captivating tour through the cutting edge of technology while analysing how AI affects the complex web of international financial transactions. As we stand at the threshold of a new age, this book aims to explore the layers of complexity underlying the confluence of AI and remittances. Our investigation goes beyond the current state of affairs and into the future, whereby predictive analytics and autonomous financial transactions will fundamentally alter the way that we send and receive money internationally.

This investigation began with the realisation that remittances are more than just money transfers—they are vital links that maintain communities, bind families together and promote economic development. The incorporation of AI technology into this process represents a revolution rather than a simple progression, one that might improve millions of people's lives by streamlining, securing and lowering the cost of financial transactions. In these pages, we break down the complex workings of artificial intelligence (AI) prediction models, reveal how blockchain integration may be used to facilitate safe and transparent transactions and examine how biometric authentication can strengthen the security of financial transactions. We dive into the complexities of regulatory compliance, understanding the difficult balance between innovation and conformity to existing standards.

We also ask you to consider a future in which artificial intelligence (AI) governs autonomous financial transactions. When machines carry out transactions based on complex algorithms and current market circumstances, what does it entail for people and economies? What effect does this change have on how people make financial decisions? *Redefining Cross-Border Financial Flows* is an invitation to imagine a future in which financial systems are not just efficient but also naturally intelligent rather than merely an examination of the possibilities. It is a call to reflect on the moral ramifications, the effects on society and the obligations that accompany the dawn of a new era of financial opportunity. We want you to explore the revolutionary concepts provided in the pages that follow by asking questions, thinking critically and participating in the journey. Remittances are about to undergo a revolution, and you have a crucial role to play in determining how this will play out.

Abbreviations

AI	Artificial Intelligence
AML	Anti-Money Laundering
CBDCs	Central Bank Digital Currencies
CDD	Customer Due Diligence
CTF	Counter-Terrorism Financing
DAOs	Decentralised Autonomous Organisations
DDoS	Distributed Denial of Service
DeFi	Decentralised Finance
DEXs	Decentralised Exchanges
EWallets	Electronic Wallets
FATF	Financial Action Task Force
GDPR	General Data Protection Regulation
KYC	Know Your Customer
NLP	Natural Language Processing
P2P	Peer-to-Peer
RegTech	Regulatory Technology

Introduction

The combination of artificial intelligence (AI) with the banking sector has revolutionised cross-border money transfers and management in an era of unparalleled technical breakthroughs. Thanks to artificial intelligence (AI) innovation, the global remittance sector, which provides a crucial lifeline for millions of people, is experiencing a significant upheaval. *Redefining Cross-Border Financial Flows: Transforming Remittances with AI and Other Technologies* takes readers on a tour of this vibrant junction where innovation converges to fulfil the pressing demands of business and society. There has never been a greater need for quick, safe and affordable cross-border transactions as the globe grows more linked. This book weaves together the threads of sophisticated predictive models, blockchain integration, biometric verification and the changing environment of autonomous financial transactions to examine the complex picture of AI's impact on remittances. We expose the many levels of complexity that will influence how financial transfers are shaped in the future through a thorough investigation of these cutting-edge technologies.

This volume's contents go beyond the traditional remittance conversation bounds and explore data analytics, machine learning and regulatory compliance. We explore the subtleties of how AI-powered algorithms forecast currency changes and provide people the best times to transfer money to get the most out of their hard-earned cash. Blockchain technology integration shines as a ray of hope, guaranteeing transactions are transparent, traceable and safe. As we analyse the function of fingerprint scans and face recognition in bolstering the security of remittance transactions, biometric authentication takes the stage.

The book sheds light on how these technologies serve as watchful defenders against the constantly changing world of financial crime in addition to verifying users.

In addition, *Redefining Cross-Border Financial Flows* looks ahead, imagining a financial environment in which AI performs transactions on its own, following predetermined rules and taking into account current market circumstances. This futuristic look explores the possibilities for previously unheard-of precision and efficiency while also posing concerns about the changing role of people in financial transactions. We traverse the regulatory waterways that oversee international financial transactions across these pages. In a globally integrated financial environment, AI-driven analytics emerges as the key to compliance, guaranteeing adherence to Know Your Customer (KYC) and Anti-Money Laundering (AML) rules.

CHAPTER 1

Remittance Revolution

In an age characterised by lightning-fast technical progress, the financial sector is undergoing a revolutionary upheaval, especially when it comes to cross-border transactions. Remittances are more than simply cash transactions for millions of people worldwide; they are lifelines that span national boundaries and are intertwined with strands of love, duty and hope. Every relocation, no matter how big or small, represents the weight of hopes abandoned, families split up and aspirations fostered from a distance. However, the route these essential resources traverse is frequently paved with obstacles, inefficiencies and unstated expenses.

Redefining Cross-Border Financial Flows: Transforming Remittances with AI and Other Technology, a book, explores the dynamic relationship between artificial intelligence (AI) and the international remittance sector. The first chapter establishes the framework for our investigation.

Definition of Remittances

Remittances are essentially the monetary transactions carried out by persons who are employed in foreign nations to send money back to their country of origin. These transfers are not simply transactions; they represent the hopes, efforts and family ties of millions around the globe. Remittances are vital for several economies, since they offer essential nutrition and assistance to families, promote education and stimulate local economies.

© Hari Prasad Josyula 2024
H. P. Josyula, *Redefining Cross-Border Financial Flows,*
https://doi.org/10.1007/979-8-8688-1064-0_1

Remittances, which refer to the monetary transfers made by migrants from the nations they are residing in to their countries of origin, play a crucial role in the functioning of the global economy. By 2023, it is estimated that they would achieve an astonishing $800 billion, overtaking foreign direct investment as the primary source of external funding for emerging nations. These grants support several objectives, promoting rural development, encouraging entrepreneurship and enhancing access to education and healthcare for millions of people. Remittances encompass more than just numerical figures; they represent narratives of determination, selflessness and an unwavering aspiration for a more promising tomorrow. These stories range from the construction of educational institutions in isolated communities to the empowerment of women via microfinance.

Significance in the Global Economy

The role of remittances in the global economy cannot be emphasised. Aside from the family impact, these money infusions play an important role in developing national economies. According to the World Bank, remittances to low- and middle-income countries will total $540 billion in 2020, more than foreign direct investment and government development aid combined. This financial lifeline supports communities, reduces poverty and promotes global economic progress.

Remittances have a far-reaching influence that goes beyond economic metrics, permeating the social fabric of communities everywhere. They cross great physical distances, keeping families together and sparking intergenerational solidarity. Remittances provide displaced people with a sense of action and control, reminding them that their efforts have an influence even from a distance. They cultivate hope and resilience, moving families up the development ladder and leaving an unforgettable imprint on the global development scene.

Overview of Traditional Cross-Border Transactions

Cross-border transactions have always been associated with high expenses, protracted processing delays and inherent inefficiencies. These transactions are complicated and can cause financial hardships for both senders and receivers. Problems with currency conversion combined with middleman costs make it difficult for money to move smoothly across borders. In this situation, promoting financial inclusion and accelerating economic growth need not just a desired but also an essential paradigm change. But inaccessibility creates another level of difficulty, especially in rural locations where senders have fewer alternatives and must deal with inconvenient scheduling. The safety of these transactions is also a continuous worry because migrant populations are often targets of fraud and scams.

The Need for Transformation

The constraints imposed by conventional systems highlight the need for change in the field of cross-border financial flows. The shortcomings of current models are exacerbated as the world economy grows more integrated. The desire for innovation is a resounding demand from people, businesses and entire economies; it is not only an echo in the hallways of financial institutions.

The need to address problems like exorbitant transaction prices, sluggish processing times and accessibility concerns is what drives the need for reform. The need for effective, safe and cutting-edge technical solutions is growing as the globe grows more linked. This book sets out to investigate how artificial intelligence (AI) technology, with its plethora of applications, may lead this change and completely reshape the world of international financial transactions.

Remittances are more than simply financial transactions, despite AI's unmatched promises of speed and security. They are infused with personal narratives, sentimental bonds and a fundamental need for human connection. Together, digital innovators, policy leaders, financial institutions and, most crucially, the voices of migrants and their families must embark on this revolutionary journey. We can rewrite the story of remittances and usher in a new age where every transfer represents not just monetary worth but also the unending love, optimism and resilience that propels the travels of millions of people around the globe by embracing a human-centric approach and utilising AI.

CHAPTER 2

Understanding Remittance Challenges

A thorough grasp of the obstacles that have impeded remittance operations in the past is essential in the dynamic world of cross-border commerce. The terrain of cross-border financial contacts between people is constantly changing due to a variety of variables, including economic developments and technology breakthroughs. Understanding the complexities and past obstacles associated with remittance systems is essential to negotiating the transition to a more technologically sophisticated, inclusive and effective future.

Since they allow for distant family ties and financial support, remittances have played a crucial role in human history. Nevertheless, there have always been difficulties with the past methods used to carry out these transfers. Time-consuming processing delays, complicated currency exchange rates, expensive transaction fees and restricted accessibility have all frequently occurred as barriers to the efficient movement of cash.

The historical difficulties with remittance procedures have significant economic ramifications in addition to being minor annoyances. For example, high transaction fees cause a large amount of money to be diverted from their intended use, which reduces the beneficial effects remittances may have on recipient families' financial stability. Prolonged processing periods may result in postponed financial assistance, impeding urgent needs and perhaps stopping business ventures that depend on prompt funding.

© Hari Prasad Josyula 2024
H. P. Josyula, *Redefining Cross-Border Financial Flows*,
https://doi.org/10.1007/979-8-8688-1064-0_2

High Transaction Costs

Remittances have significant challenges due to high transaction costs, which put a financial strain on both senders and receivers. This widespread problem, which has its roots in the conventional banking system, has important economic ramifications and highlights the pressing need for innovative solutions.

High transaction costs are essentially the fees and charges related to international money transfers. Conventional remittance routes sometimes entail a convoluted web of middlemen, each of whom charges a fee. These costs might include transfer fees, currency translation fees and even unstated expenses incurred throughout the remittance process. Remittances have a negative effect on the financial stability of families and communities as a result of a significant amount of the money meant for beneficiaries being embezzled.

High transaction costs have significant economic ramifications that go well beyond simple remittance transfers. The money that is diverted and used to pay transaction fees may be used for other important expenses like local business ventures, healthcare or education. Therefore, the continuation of high transaction costs hinders the revolutionary potential that remittances carry for economic growth and feeds a vicious cycle of financial pressure.

The inefficiency of conventional banking systems and the absence of competition in the remittance industry are the two main drivers of high transaction costs. Along the remittance path, intermediaries add layers of fees that are frequently opaque and challenging for the sender and receiver to understand. The total cost of the transaction is further increased by foreign conversion rates, which are occasionally marked up by these middlemen. As a result, a system that takes advantage of the opaqueness is created, keeping senders and receivers in the dark about the actual expenses associated with remitting money.

But this difficulty also presents a chance for creativity. Blockchain and cryptocurrency, in particular, are emerging technologies that have shown promise in lowering remittance transaction costs. Because blockchain is transparent and decentralised, it can reduce the number of middlemen required and the levels of costs associated with the transfer process. With its use of blockchain technology, cryptocurrencies provide a substitute for conventional remittance routes, enabling quicker and more affordable cross-border transfers.

In addition, the emergence of fintech firms that focus on digital remittance solutions has created competition in the market, forcing established banking institutions to review their charge schedules. These online platforms employ technology to improve overall efficiency, lower expenses and streamline procedures, giving customers easier access to and a lower cost of remittance services.

It is essential to take into account the effects on the most disadvantaged people while attempting to solve high transaction costs. The majority of these expenses may fall on migrant labourers, who are frequently the main remittance senders. The share of earnings that transaction fees take from people who work in low-paying occupations overseas can be disproportionately large. This fact underscores the need for comprehensive solutions that put the financial security of those who depend on remittances as a primary means of supporting their family back home first.

The way that remittances are shaped is also greatly influenced by governmental and regulatory entities. Transparency, competition and the uptake of cutting-edge technology are all factors that can lower transaction costs. International cooperation to set norms for fees and remittance procedures can promote a more standardised and economical system that benefits senders and receivers anywhere in the world.

As we manage the complexity of high transaction costs in remittances, it is crucial to imagine a future where financial inclusion is not impeded by costly fees. Using technology to build a more open, effective and accessible remittance environment has the potential to be revolutionary. Blockchain technology, cryptocurrencies and the creative methods used by fintech businesses provide a window into a future in which people will be able to send and receive money internationally at a fair price and with little difficulty.

Remittances' high transaction costs, however, pose a complex problem with wide-ranging economic effects. But this difficulty also presents a chance for creativity and change. In the future, remittances will not only be more affordable, but they will also be a significant driver of global financial inclusion and economic growth if the banking sector embraces innovative technology, encourages competition and puts inclusive laws into place.

Slow Processing Times

The delayed processing of remittances poses a major obstacle to the prompt and effective transfer of cash across international borders. This widespread problem, which has its roots in antiquated banking systems, not only causes annoyance to senders and recipients but also has significant negative economic effects. In order to expedite cross-border transactions, this investigation will explore the complex dynamics of long processing times, looking at the reasons behind them, their effects on the economy and possible fixes.

In essence, sluggish processing times are the delays that occur while money is being sent from the sender to the receiver. A number of middlemen, each in charge of confirming and assisting the transaction, are frequently involved in traditional remittance systems. These transactions are slow in part because of the bureaucratic procedures, outdated systems and strict legal restrictions. As a result, the intended recipients—who frequently want financial assistance immediately—experience delays in receiving the sent monies.

Processing times that are too sluggish have wide-ranging and complex economic consequences. For recipients who depend on timely cash to satisfy basic requirements like healthcare, education and everyday costs, delayed remittances can have dire consequences. Additionally, a halt in the flow of cash can negatively impact economic activity on both ends, since postponed capital infusions can stifle regional initiative and economic expansion.

The old banking infrastructure is firmly ingrained with the core reasons of sluggish processing times. The lengthy processing times are caused in part by the requirement for several levels of verification, compliance audits and a lack of interoperability between financial institutions. The system's inefficiencies are further compounded by the dependence on antiquated technology and manual procedures.

On the other hand, new technologies provide workable ways to speed up remittance processing times. Because blockchain technology is decentralised and transparent, it can expedite the verification process by giving everyone involved access to a single, unchangeable record. By automating the validation and release of cash, smart contracts—self-executing contracts with the rules of the agreement explicitly put into code—can drastically cut down on processing times.

In order to solve lengthy processing times, fintech businesses that specialise in digital remittance platforms have also been instrumental. These systems use contemporary technology to streamline and automate the remittance process at every step, from cash transfer to identity verification. Because of this, transactions using digital remittance solutions may be completed almost instantly, unlike through traditional methods, which have longer lead times.

Furthermore, remittance procedures can be accelerated by financial institutions working together and being interoperable. Standardised communication routes and protocols can facilitate a more smooth information flow, cutting down on the amount of time needed for validation and verification. Global programmes that encourage this kind of cooperation can open the door to a cross-border payment environment that is more integrated and effective.

Another important factor in overcoming delayed processing times is the involvement of governmental and regulatory authorities. Clear and simplified regulatory frameworks may offer the required advice for financial institutions to utilise contemporary technology without sacrificing compliance. The remittance environment may change even more quickly if there are incentives for adopting creative solutions and getting rid of red tape.

One way to understand the human aspect of this problem is to look at how delayed processing times affect migrant workers, who are frequently the main remittance senders. Remittances are essential to the financial support of migrant workers, many of whom choose low-paying employment overseas, and their family back home. Fund transfer delays might make migrants feel more financially stressed and make it more difficult for them to take care of their families.

In conclusion, remittance processing delays are a complex issue that need for an all-encompassing and creative solution. Accelerating cross-border transactions requires addressing the underlying causes, embracing emerging technologies, fostering collaboration and streamlining regulatory frameworks. With the combined efforts of the banking sector, digital companies and government agencies, a future where remittances operate smoothly, supporting beneficiaries on time and fostering economic growth, is attainable.

Currency Exchange Issues

Issues with currency exchange pose a serious threat to cross-border transactions, impacting the effectiveness and value of remittances. This complicated issue includes changes in exchange rates, related costs and the general difficulty of negotiating several currency systems. We will examine the economic ramifications of currency conversion problems, the mechanics of exchange rate swings, possible technical solutions and the significance of promoting openness in the remittance process as we dig into the complexities of these issues.

The difficulty of managing exchange rate variations is at the core of currency exchange problems. Currency prices fluctuate often due to a number of reasons, such as market emotion, geopolitical events and economic data. Remittance values are at risk due to these changes, which affect senders and receivers equally. The recipient can get less than what the sender had meant to send when the exchange rate is bad at the time of the transaction.

Currency exchange problems have significant economic ramifications that go beyond individual transactions. Exchange rate fluctuations add a degree of uncertainty, making it difficult for senders and receivers to project with precision how much will be received in the end. Financial planning may be hampered by this uncertainty, especially for recipients who rely on remittances to cover everyday expenses, healthcare and educational costs.

The difficulties are made even more difficult by associated currency exchange expenses. Currency conversion fees are sometimes charged extra through traditional remittance methods, and these costs can mount up. Remittance value can be greatly reduced by the combined effect of exchange rate changes and related fees, which can have an adverse effect on recipients' buying power and restrict the beneficial effects of these financial inflows on local economies.

Exchange rate variations are highly challenging to anticipate due to their complicated dynamics, which are impacted by several factors. Currency prices fluctuate due to a variety of factors, including interest rates, market sentiment, economic data and geopolitical developments. Currency exchange is traditionally handled by centralised middlemen who may markup exchange rates to offset their expenses and make a profit. The difficulties presented by currency conversion problems can be exacerbated by this lack of transparency in the exchange process, which may result in unintended expenses for senders and receivers.

New technologies, like blockchain and cryptocurrencies, provide creative ways to deal with the problems associated with currency conversion in remittances. Exchange rates may be reflected more accurately and instantly because to blockchain's decentralised and transparent structure. Blockchain can help create more equitable and reliable currency trades by removing the need for several middlemen and increasing process transparency.

Based on blockchain technology, cryptocurrencies provide a decentralised, international method of value transmission. Exchange rate swings can be lessened by using stablecoins, a class of cryptocurrencies linked to the value of conventional fiat money. Senders and receivers may be able to circumvent the volatility linked to traditional currencies by employing stablecoins as a middleman in the remittance process.

Peer-to-peer (P2P) networks and digital wallet use can also expedite the currency conversion procedure. These platforms employ technology to connect buyers and sellers of money at competitive rates, frequently giving consumers better terms. P2P systems are more efficient and economical because of their automated and decentralised structure, which also lessens the friction involved in using conventional cash exchange techniques.

Addressing currency exchange concerns requires promoting openness in the remittance process. Senders and receivers may make educated judgements when exchange rates and related costs are communicated clearly. Transparency is a top priority for fintech businesses that specialise in digital remittance platforms, giving consumers access to up-to-date information on costs and currency rates. Users are empowered by this openness, which also helps to increase remittance process confidence.

The environment around currency exchange in remittances is significantly shaped by governmental and regulatory entities. To address currency exchange concerns, policies that support openness, equitable competition and the deployment of cutting-edge technologies might be helpful. International cooperation to create guidelines for remittance currency conversion can promote a more standardised and open system that is advantageous to senders and receivers alike.

The complexity of currency conversion problems affects the effectiveness and value of remittances in cross-border transactions. The need for creative solutions is highlighted by the economic ramifications, which are fueled by fees and volatility in currency rates. Blockchain and cryptocurrency are examples of emerging technologies that present possible solutions to these problems by offering efficiency, transparency and the possibility to lessen the effects of fluctuating exchange rates. Encouraging remittance process transparency in conjunction with legislative frameworks that are supportive can help create a more inclusive and fairer environment for families and people who depend on cross-border financial flows.

Accessibility and Inclusivity

Accessibility and inclusion are key factors in cross-border transactions, particularly remittances. This multidimensional problem centres around ensuring that financial services are accessible to all people, regardless of their geographical location, economic position or access to traditional banking channels. As we delve into the complexities of remittance accessibility and inclusivity, we will look at the barriers that different segments of the population face, the role of technology in promoting greater financial inclusion and the significance of regulatory frameworks that prioritise equitable access to financial services.

At its root, the existence of unbanked and underbanked communities creates a problem for remittance accessibility and inclusion. Millions of people worldwide lack access to conventional financial channels, making it impossible for them to send or receive remittances using traditional methods. The unbanked, who sometimes live in distant or rural locations, face challenges such as restricted physical access to banks, insufficient documentation and a lack of financial awareness. In contrast, the underbanked may have access to basic financial services but are nevertheless cut off from the larger financial ecosystem.

Migrants, who are among the top remittance senders, frequently experience accessibility issues. Many migrant workers work in low-wage occupations overseas and may not have access to standard financial services. Additionally, the absence of banking infrastructure in their native nations might restrict the ease with which recipients obtain remitted monies. Bridging the accessibility gap for migrant workers is critical since their financial well-being and capacity to support their family are dependent on the speed and inclusiveness of the remittance process.

Technological improvements are critical in tackling the issues of accessibility and inclusiveness in remittances. The growth of mobile technology and digital financial platforms has allowed for new solutions that reach people outside the traditional banking infrastructure. Mobile money services, for example, enable customers to send and receive dollars via simple mobile phones, removing the requirement for a traditional bank account. This discovery has been especially beneficial in areas with strong mobile phone adoption but limited access to conventional banking institutions.

Moreover, fintech businesses specialised in digital remittance platforms employ technology to build user-friendly interfaces and speed the transfer process. The digitalisation of remittances not only increases accessibility but also lowers the costs associated with traditional channels, making financial services more accessible to a larger part of the population. Digital wallets and peer-to-peer platforms help to increase financial inclusion by offering alternatives to the conventional banking industry and meeting the requirements of the unbanked and underbanked.

Regulatory frameworks are critical in determining the landscape of accessibility and inclusiveness in remittances. Governments and regulatory organisations may either help or impede financial inclusion through their policies. Progressive policies that welcome digital financial innovations, protect consumers and promote competition can create an atmosphere favourable to increased accessibility. In contrast, regulatory barriers, a lack of transparency and onerous criteria can stymie the adoption of technology-driven solutions, limiting their reach and effect.

The importance of promoting financial awareness and education cannot be emphasised in the pursuit of inclusion. Many people, particularly in impoverished places, may he unfamlliar with digital financial services and the benefits they may provide. Educational activities may help people use digital platforms with confidence, understand security measures and make educated financial decisions. Bridging the knowledge gap helps to develop confidence in digital financial solutions, which encourages their wider adoption.

In order to achieve accessibility and inclusion, it is critical to recognise the distinct demands of various demographic groups. Women, for example, may encounter additional challenges owing to sociocultural constraints, limited mobility or a lack of documents. Tailoring financial solutions to women's unique concerns promotes inclusion and ensures that the advantages of remittances reach all members of a community.

Global cooperation and partnerships also help to promote accessibility and inclusiveness in remittances. Cross-border transactions necessitate financial system interoperability, and international collaboration can result in process and technology standardisation. Initiatives that encourage collaboration between financial institutions, technology suppliers and regulatory authorities assist in establishing a more integrated and inclusive global financial ecosystem.

Accessibility and inclusiveness in remittances are critical components of developing a financial environment that meets the different needs of individuals and communities globally. The issues posed by the unbanked, underbanked, migrants and other disadvantaged communities highlight the importance of implementing inclusive solutions. Technology, with its ability to bridge gaps and give user-friendly alternatives, serves as a catalyst for change. Regulatory frameworks that encourage innovation while prioritising consumer safety help to create an environment in which financial services are accessible to everyone. As we traverse the intricacies of financial inclusion, we must recognise the diversity of demands and develop solutions that empower individuals, enabling a future in which everyone has equal access to the advantages of cross-border financial transactions.

CHAPTER 3

The Role of AI in Financial Technology

The confluence of increased processing power, complex algorithms and vast databases has created a new era in banking, where robots are not simply tools but intelligent partners. Artificial intelligence (AI) has become an integral part of financial technology, changing how we view, engage with and negotiate the intricate world of financial transactions.

In its most basic form, artificial intelligence (AI) is the simulation of human intellect by computers, allowing them to comprehend enormous volumes of data, learn from it, adapt and make defensible judgements. This intelligence translates into a wide range of applications in the field of financial technology that go much beyond conventional paradigms.

Artificial intelligence (AI) has impacted every aspect of financial operations, including risk management, fraud detection, investment strategies and credit scoring. Artificial intelligence (AI) has become incredibly important due to its machines' capacity to analyse patterns, derive insights and forecast events at a speed and precision that is not possible with conventional approaches.

© Hari Prasad Josyula 2024
H. P. Josyula, *Redefining Cross-Border Financial Flows*,
https://doi.org/10.1007/979-8-8688-1064-0_3

Overview of Artificial Intelligence

One of the most significant and disruptive technical developments of our day is artificial intelligence (AI), which is changing whole economies, industries and even the way we live our everyday lives. The creation of computer systems that are capable of activities that normally require human intelligence is the essence of artificial intelligence (AI). This explores the vast and complex field of artificial intelligence (AI), offering a thorough synopsis that includes its background, essential elements, uses and the significant influence it has had on other fields, with a particular emphasis on financial technology.

The study of machine intelligence and attempts to mimic human cognitive processes lay the foundation for artificial intelligence (AI), which began in the middle of the 20th century. The theoretical groundwork for artificial intelligence (AI) was established by early pioneers like Alan Turing and John McCarthy, who envisioned robots that might replicate human intellect. However, AI didn't really start to reach its potential until the development of powerful computers and the accessibility of enormous datasets.

AI is made up of a wide range of technologies, each of which adds to its overall capabilities in a distinct way. Without explicit programming, machine learning, a subset of artificial intelligence, allows computers to learn from data and gradually improve their performance. The foundation of AI systems' adaptability and dynamic nature is this iterative learning process. By enabling robots to comprehend, interpret and produce human language, natural language processing, or NLP, improves human-machine communication. Through computer vision, robots can comprehend and 'see' the environment in a manner similar to human vision by interpreting visual data.

AI has several uses in a variety of areas, including healthcare, education, manufacturing and finance. AI has changed the game in the financial industry by bringing efficiencies, streamlining procedures and opening up new avenues. The use of artificial intelligence (AI) in financial technology, or fintech, has completely changed how people interact with their finances, how financial institutions function and how transactions are carried out.

Machine learning is one of the main tenets of AI in fintech. Financial systems can now analyse enormous volumes of data to find trends, forecast outcomes and streamline decision-making procedures because of this technology. Machine learning models use past data in risk management to anticipate and reduce possible dangers, improving the precision of risk assessments. Fraud detection systems use machine learning algorithms to instantly spot potentially fraudulent activity and identify abnormal trends.

The emergence of robo-advisors, AI-powered systems that evaluate market trends, risk profiles and individual preferences to offer individualised financial advice, has revolutionised the field of investment management. By making complex investing methods available to a wider public, these robo-advisors democratise access to financial advice. Algorithmic trading is a financial application of artificial intelligence that utilises real-time data analysis and optimisation algorithms to perform high-frequency transactions at a pace that is unattainable for human traders.

AI has revolutionised credit rating, a crucial component of financial transactions. In order to evaluate a person's creditworthiness more thoroughly, machine learning algorithms examine a variety of data sources, including non-traditional indications like social media engagement and online behaviour. By going above and beyond standard credit scoring techniques, this inclusive approach gives those who would have been turned away based on conventional criteria access to financial possibilities.

Another example of AI in fintech is the development of chatbots and virtual assistants, which improve client interactions and expedite customer care procedures. Natural language processing is used by these AI-driven interfaces to comprehend and reply to client inquiries, offering immediate assistance and information. The integration of artificial intelligence (AI) with customer relationship management (CRM) systems allows financial organisations to provide tailored and prompt services, resulting in improved client experiences.

AI's influence on cross-border transactions is growing as it continues to enter the financial sector. AI plays a major role in tackling issues related to currency exchange, transaction security, market volatility and regulatory compliance in the global financial arena because of its capacity to handle enormous datasets and produce insightful results.

AI Applications in Finance

In the financial industry, artificial intelligence (AI) has become a keystone, transforming how organisations function, make decisions and interact with their clientele. This examines the various uses of AI in finance, including credit scoring, risk management, fraud detection, investment management and customer support. An age of unmatched efficiency, precision and creativity has been brought about by the integration of AI with financial technology, or fintech, which has transformed conventional procedures and created new opportunities for financial institutions.

Risk management is one of the most important areas where artificial intelligence is being used in finance. Large-scale datasets are analysed by AI algorithms to anticipate and reduce possible dangers, improving the precision of risk evaluations. Through the use of machine learning models, financial institutions may get insights about anticipated market swings, credit risks and other variables that may affect their portfolios by identifying patterns and anomalies in historical data. AI's dynamic and adaptable characteristics make it a valuable tool for managing risk in an ever-evolving financial environment.

Artificial intelligence has become a reliable defender against financial fraud. With the use of machine learning algorithms that can recognise patterns, transaction data is continually analysed to look for unusual trends that might point to fraud. Artificial intelligence (AI)-driven fraud detection systems are capable of spotting abnormalities in real time, whether they are related to identity theft, unauthorised access or sophisticated schemes. This allows financial institutions to take prompt action to safeguard their clients and assets.

AI is having a revolutionary impact on investment management, especially in light of the introduction of robo-advisors. These artificial intelligence (AI) platforms use algorithms to assess risk profiles, market trends and user preferences in order to provide tailored investing recommendations. Robo-advisors provide accessibility to complex investing methods by democratising them for a wider range of users. These systems' algorithms are capable of optimising investment portfolios using real-time market data, making deft judgements faster than a person could.

In the financial markets, algorithmic trading is a common use of artificial intelligence. High-frequency trading is made possible by AI-driven algorithms' speed and accuracy, which allow transactions to be executed at frequencies and speeds that are not feasible for human traders. These algorithms optimise investment portfolios and react quickly to market volatility by analysing market circumstances, spotting opportunities and executing trades in real time. A key component of contemporary financial markets, algorithmic trading affects liquidity and shapes trading tactics.

AI has brought about a revolution in credit scoring, moving beyond traditional approaches to analyse an individual's creditworthiness more fully. Diverse data points, including non-traditional indicators like social media activity and online behaviour, are analysed using machine learning algorithms. People who may be turned down for credit based on traditional credit scoring standards now have access to financial possibilities thanks to this comprehensive methodology, which enables a more nuanced assessment. An evaluation of a person's financial situation that is more accurate and inclusive is made possible by AI-driven credit scoring.

The banking industry's customer service has changed with the introduction of AI. Natural language processing-capable chatbots and virtual assistants offer prompt and helpful customer service. These AI-powered user interfaces are able to comprehend and interpret user inquiries and provide transactional services as well as help and information. Financial institutions may provide efficient and personalised client experiences through the integration of AI with CRM systems, which raises customer happiness and engagement levels.

It is impossible to overestimate the influence of AI applications on customer happiness, cost reduction and operational efficiency as they continue to spread throughout the financial industry. AI is ideally suited for solving intricate problems and revealing insightful information because of the financial markets' dynamic character and the massive volumes of data they create. Artificial intelligence (AI) is a potent ally in negotiating the complexities of the financial world because of the mutually beneficial link between human knowledge and machine intelligence.

Regarding AI's potential in banking, the applications covered here are just the tip of the iceberg. Artificial intelligence is revolutionising financial institutions' operations and client interactions, from automated decision-making to predictive analytics. As we get further into the upcoming chapters, we'll concentrate on AI's involvement in cross-border transactions, examining how its capabilities change the face of global financial flows and support an international financial ecosystem that is safer, more effective and more inclusive.

Benefits of AI in Cross-Border Transactions

Artificial intelligence (AI) is a disruptive force in the world of cross-border transactions, providing several benefits that redefine the efficiency, security and general dynamics of international financial flows. This article delves into the significant benefits that AI provides to cross-border transactions, including advanced prediction models, increased security measures, hyper-personalisation and the transition to autonomous financial transactions.

One of the key advantages of using AI in cross-border transactions is the creation of improved prediction models. AI's ability to handle large amounts of information and identify patterns enables the development of sophisticated models for predicting currency exchange rates. This technology helps to mitigate the risks associated with currency rate swings, allowing enterprises and people to optimise the timing of cross-border transactions. Using predictive analytics, stakeholders may make educated decisions about when and how to perform transactions, reducing the effect of adverse exchange rate swings.

The integration of AI with blockchain technology represents a significant step forward in assuring the security and transparency of cross-border transactions. Blockchain, with its decentralised and immutable record, provides a safe and transparent platform for financial transactions. AI algorithms supplement this by validating and analysing transactions, which improves the integrity of financial data. The marriage of AI with blockchain not only lowers the danger of fraud, but it also increases trust between transacting parties. This integration's openness and security are especially important in cross-border transactions, which entail varied regulatory regimes and complicated networks of intermediaries.

AI's use of natural language processing (NLP) and sentiment analysis helps to better comprehend market sentiments in cross-border transactions. AI can evaluate market mood in real time by analysing enormous volumes of news, social media and financial statistics. This feature provides decision-makers with information on probable market movements, geopolitical events and economic data that might affect currency prices. Integrating NLP and sentiment analysis into cross-border transaction strategies enables stakeholders to make educated decisions based on current sentiment in global financial markets.

The security of cross-border transactions is critical, and AI plays an important role in this arena by integrating biometric authentication and enhanced fraud protection methods. Biometric authentication, such as fingerprint or face recognition, provides an additional layer of security by guaranteeing that only authorised users may begin and approve transactions. AI-powered fraud protection algorithms are constantly evolving to uncover new patterns of fraudulent activity, allowing real-time detection and prevention. This not only protects the financial interests of individuals and businesses doing cross-border transactions, but it also helps to establish confidence in the wider financial ecosystem.

AI's capacity to analyse large datasets enables hyper-personalisation in cross-border transactions. AI customises services based on transaction histories, spending habits and customer preferences. This goes beyond mere customisation to give a highly personalised experience for users doing cross-border financial transactions. Hyper-personalisation not only improves customer happiness, but it also helps to produce customer-centric financial products and services that respond to the specific needs of various user segments participating in international transactions.

AI-driven analytics in cross-border transactions help to simplify the complicated environment of regulatory compliance. AI algorithms enable compliance with changing rules by automating compliance operations and monitoring transactions for possible regulatory hazards. The ability of AI to process and analyse large amounts of data in real time allows financial institutions to stay current on regulatory changes and adjust their operations accordingly. This not only decreases the risk of noncompliance, but it also improves cross-border transaction efficiency by reducing delays and assuring regulatory compliance.

AI's analytical skills include real-time market insights and worldwide remittance patterns, which influence strategic decision-making in cross-border transactions. Predictive analytics based on historical data allows stakeholders to anticipate market trends and optimise resource allocation. Understanding global remittance patterns enables financial institutions and enterprises to tailor their strategies to the changing demands and preferences of cross-border financial customers. AI-powered analytics give insights that help businesses be agile and adaptable in the face of changing market conditions.

One of the most futuristic advantages of AI in cross-border transactions is the transition to autonomous financial transactions. AI algorithms, via continual learning and modification, have the capacity to carry out transactions independently. This notion anticipates a future in which financial transactions are optimised, performed and completed without requiring direct human interaction. The transition to autonomous financial transactions provides the potential for unprecedented efficiency, lower costs and faster cross-border financial activity.

The benefits of AI in cross-border transactions are far-reaching, affecting everything from security and transparency to customer experience and strategic planning. As stakeholders across the financial ecosystem embrace AI capabilities, the landscape of international financial flows evolves, providing a glimpse into a future in which transactions are not only secure and efficient but also tailored to the specific needs of users engaging in cross-border financial activities.

CHAPTER 4

Innovations in Remittance Platforms

The development of remittance platforms in the dynamic world of cross-border transactions is evidence of the financial industry's unwavering commitment to innovation. The remittance sector has experienced a dramatic transformation. Historically, it has been defined by its dependence on broad networks of intermediaries and traditional banking channels. Advances in technology, together with the introduction of blockchain and artificial intelligence (AI), have opened the door to a new age in remittance systems.

Remittance platforms' digitalisation signifies a significant departure from conventional approaches, which frequently incurred delays and extra expenses due to the presence of physical infrastructure and middlemen. Modern technology is used by digital remittance platforms to improve security, expedite procedures and provide customers with unmatched control over their financial transactions. The use of blockchain and decentralised ledger technology is fundamental to the advancements in remittance platform innovation. The irreversible nature of blockchain protects the security and transparency of transactions, minimising the dangers associated with fraud and unauthorised access. Because these systems are decentralised, there is no longer a need for middlemen, which lowers transaction costs and quickens the pace at which money may move across borders.

© Hari Prasad Josyula 2024
H. P. Josyula, *Redefining Cross-Border Financial Flows*,
https://doi.org/10.1007/979-8-8688-1064-0_4

Advanced Predictive Models

The use of advanced predictive models is key to the remittance platforms' revolutionary path. These models herald in a new era of data-driven decision-making, driven by advanced algorithms and machine learning capabilities. Predictive models, with their capacity to evaluate past data, spot trends and project future trends, are a priceless aid in managing the intricacies of international trade.

The use of predictive models in remittances signals a fundamental change in the way international financial transactions are carried out. These models predict several aspects of cross-border financial operations by using market trends, user behaviour and historical transaction data. The applications are numerous and significant, ranging from forecasting currency exchange rates to anticipating transaction processing times. By utilising predictive models, consumers and service providers may obtain insights beyond simple historical analysis, empowering them to make well-informed decisions instantly.

The incorporation of predictive analytics for transaction optimisation emerges as a cornerstone in boosting the efficiency and cost-effectiveness of remittances. Remittance platforms are able to optimise several elements of transactions thanks to predictive analytics, which is powered by sophisticated models. This includes figuring out the best times to convert currencies to reduce volatility in exchange rates, figuring out the cheapest ways to send money and even projecting when processing times could take longer than expected. As previously discussed, the combination of transaction optimisation and predictive analytics not only improves efficiency but also makes cross-border financial transactions more frictionless and user-friendly.

The ability of sophisticated models to forecast future events is especially important in the field of remittances, where even little changes in exchange rates can have a big financial impact. Predictive analytics can provide financial institutions, service providers and users with the kind of foresight that will turn cross-border transactions from reactive to proactive and strategic initiatives.

Predictive model dynamics in remittances go beyond simple data analysis. Over time, these models constantly improve their prediction powers by actively learning and adapting. The models record and examine transaction patterns, user preferences and market trends as consumers interact with remittance systems. The forecasts produced by this dynamic learning process are guaranteed to be dynamic and to change with the constantly shifting global financial scene.

Predicting changes in currency exchange rates is one of the main areas where predictive models excel. Conventional transfer methods sometimes exposed consumers to currency market volatility, creating uncertainty about the beneficiary's ultimate payment amount. On the other hand, sophisticated prediction models use both historical data and current market information to predict changes in currency values. By doing this, consumers may maximise their financial results and lessen the impact of market volatility by making well-informed judgements about when to start transactions.

Predictive analytics is essential for streamlining transaction processing times in addition to exchange rates. Predictive models analyse patterns in transaction lifecycles and historical data to forecast how long it will take money to go where it needs to go. Users may arrange transactions based on convenience and urgency in addition to receiving transparency and predictability from this.

The user-centric focus of the sophisticated prediction models in remittances is one of its unique characteristics. These models are intended to improve user experience overall as well as optimise backend procedures for service providers. To comprehend each user's unique behaviour, preferences and transaction history, predictive analytics is used. Remittance systems may now provide customised suggestions, including the best times to transact, routes that are least expensive and even insights into possible savings, thanks to this individualised approach.

The user-centric aspect of predictive models adds to a more engaging and empowering experience for those engaged in cross-border transactions. Predictive analytics and user-centric design work together to improve more than just transactional efficiency. It gives users a sense of control and confidence and makes the sometimes intimidating and complicated world of cross-border banking more approachable and natural.

Although the use of sophisticated prediction models in remittances offers revolutionary advantages, there are some issues that must be recognised and resolved. The financial markets' dynamic nature is one of these challenges. Unpredictability can be introduced by abrupt geopolitical events, unexpected situations or economic developments. Predictive models depend on previous data to estimate future patterns. Furthermore, a thorough analysis of the ethical issues surrounding the application of predictive analytics to financial transactions is warranted. Concerns of privacy, security and openness are critical when putting models that examine user behaviour and financial data into practice.

It also looks ahead at the complexities of sophisticated predictive algorithms in remittance systems. Predictive analytics' path in cross-border transactions is ever-changing due to continuous developments in data analytics, AI and machine learning. The changing field of predictive models, examining how new ideas and cutting-edge methods keep expanding the potential of remittance platforms. Future developments promise further sophistication and improvement, from the incorporation of real-time data feeds to the investigation of predictive models in the context of new financial instruments.

Blockchain Integration for Secure and Transparent Transactions

The incorporation of blockchain technology stands out as a disruptive force, revolutionising the way remittances are done in the fast-changing world of cross-border commerce. This section explores the significant implications of blockchain integration for safe and transparent remittance transactions, looking at its function and how it guarantees higher security and transparency in the complex international fund transfer operations.

The use of blockchain technology signifies a fundamental change in the conventional remittance platform models. Fundamentally, blockchain is a distributed, decentralised ledger that keeps track of transactions via a network of computers. The word 'blockchain' refers to the chain of blocks that are created when each transaction, contained in a block, is connected to the one before it. Because of its distributed and cryptographic design, a block added to the chain is almost unchangeable, resulting in a visible, safe and impenetrable record of transactions.

This integration creates a profound shift in the remittance situation. Cross-border transactions have traditionally included a number of middlemen, which has added complexity, caused delays and raised the possibility of fraud. By creating a peer-to-peer network and facilitating direct user transactions, blockchain expedites this procedure. This reduces the need for middlemen while guaranteeing that every transaction is safely documented on the blockchain, creating an unchangeable and visible trail.

Blockchain is more than just a ledger when it comes to remittances; it's a fundamental technology that solves major problems with conventional transfer systems. Its main function is to reduce the likelihood of fraud. Because blockchain technology is decentralised, there isn't a single point of vulnerability. Since every member of the network has a copy of the complete blockchain, it is very difficult for bad actors to change transaction data or jeopardise the system's integrity.

Furthermore, blockchain adds a level of confidence to international trade. Because they rely on centralised clearinghouses and include several middlemen, traditional systems frequently experience delays and opacity. Blockchain makes direct and transparent transactions possible with its decentralised design. Users get real-time access to transaction status tracking, providing them with insight into every phase of the process. In addition to increasing consumer trust, this transparency drastically lowers the possibility of mistakes and inconsistencies.

Blockchain's inbuilt smart contract feature makes it even more useful for remittances. Self-executing contracts, or smart contracts, have their terms encoded directly into the code. Smart contracts have the ability to automate certain parts of the transaction process in the context of remittances. For instance, the smart contract can automatically initiate the delivery of cash to the beneficiary if predetermined conditions are satisfied (such as verifying receipt of payments). This automation simplifies operations, decreases the chance of human mistake and expedites transaction settlements.

Transparency and security are critical variables in cross-border transfers, and blockchain makes sure these aspects are integrated into the remittance process rather than a merely being priority. Cryptographic techniques are employed to ensure the security of the data within each block. Because the blockchain is decentralised and every transaction is time-stamped, compromising one node does not undermine the system as a whole.

A transaction cannot be changed or removed after it has been recorded because of the blockchain's immutability. This feature assures that the transaction history cannot be tampered with and addresses data integrity problems. Customers may rely on the accuracy and lack of modification of the data stored on the blockchain.

Another essential component of blockchain integration is transparency, which completely changes the way people view and interact with international transactions. In conventional institutions, a lack of transparency regarding the flow of cash may breed mistrust and uncertainty. Blockchain helps with this by offering a traceable and transparent record of each transaction. Users get real-time insights into the status and advancement of their remittances by accessing a public ledger that traces the path of their monies.

Furthermore, blockchain's transparency has wider effects on regulatory compliance. Blockchain offers a thorough and unchangeable record, which governments and regulatory agencies are looking for in order to prevent money laundering and guarantee compliance with legislation. Remittance platforms may comply with regulations more easily as a result, and it also strengthens and increases the transparency of the global financial system.

Although there are many advantages to blockchain integration, it is crucial to recognise and manage the difficulties this technology presents when it comes to remittances. One major obstacle is scalability. Scalability becomes an important factor to take into account as blockchain technology for remittances gains traction. Traditional blockchain networks, especially public ones like Bitcoin and Ethereum, may encounter constraints in terms of transaction throughput. The techniques and ideas used to handle scalability issues are examined in this chapter, including the creation of layer-two scaling solutions and the investigation of other consensus processes.

An additional problem to take into account is interoperability. Due to their international scope, remittances frequently entail interactions between conventional financial institutions and other blockchain networks. Facilitating smooth communication between these disparate systems is essential to the general acceptance and efficacy of blockchain in remittances. This chapter explores the projects and guidelines designed to promote interoperability and build a unified ecosystem that extends beyond the confines of distinct blockchain networks.

Additionally, ethical issues are brought up, particularly in relation to user privacy. Although blockchain guarantees transaction security and transparency, concerns are raised over the persistence of personal data on the blockchain due to its irreversible nature. In order to balance the benefits of blockchain technology with the safeguarding of user privacy, this chapter examines the ethical frameworks and privacy-enhancing technologies that have been put in place.

This part lays the foundation for imagining the future trajectory of this technology as it explains the nuances of blockchain integration for safe and transparent remittance transactions. Blockchain's path in remittances is dynamic, with constant improvements and research into its full possibilities. Future developments promise even more sophistication and refinement, from the creation of next-generation blockchain networks to the incorporation of cutting-edge cryptographic algorithms.

The development of permissioned blockchains, which offer improved privacy restrictions and customised consensus processes, is one area of investigation. These blockchains are designed for certain use cases. This chapter explores the ideas and developments around permissioned blockchains and how they might be used to meet the particular needs of remittance platforms while upholding the fundamentals of security and openness.

Furthermore, new avenues for remittance innovation are made possible by the confluence of blockchain technology with other cutting-edge fields like artificial intelligence (AI) and the Internet of Things (IoT). This section looks at how blockchain and AI may work together to improve fraud detection, automate compliance procedures and maximise transaction efficiency. The relationship between blockchain technology and the Internet of Things is also explored, revealing how the combination of real-world sensor data and decentralised ledgers might provide new models for safe and open international commerce.

Natural Language Processing (NLP) and Sentiment Analysis

Sentiment analysis and natural language processing (NLP) combined are a game-changer in the complex world of cross-border finance transactions, transforming the way users engage with remittance platforms. This section explores the significant effects of sentiment analysis and natural language processing (NLP), examining how these technologies improve user experience and utilise sentiment insights to create more engaging and personalised consumer interactions in the context of international fund transfers.

Remittance platform evolution has advanced significantly with the incorporation of NLP and sentiment analysis. Natural language processing (NLP) is a branch of artificial intelligence that enables robots to comprehend, interpret and produce natural language. Contrarily, sentiment analysis employs algorithms to evaluate and ascertain the sentiment—whether positive, negative or neutral—expressed in a text. The combination of these technologies has the potential to significantly change how users interact and communicate with remittance systems.

The primary influence of natural language processing (NLP) on cross-border transactions is its ability to improve user experience. In the past, interacting with remittance platforms required interacting through structured interactions or navigating intricate interfaces. By allowing consumers to engage with remittance systems in a more conversational and natural way, NLP alters this paradigm. This segment of the talk examines how natural language processing (NLP) enables intuitive interfaces, enabling consumers to connect with remittance systems using their preferred language and even colloquial idioms.

Users may start transactions, ask questions about exchange rates and obtain personalised suggestions by integrating chatbots and virtual assistants that are powered by natural language processing (NLP) with natural language input. This simplifies the user experience and accommodates users who might not be conversant with the complexities of financial terminology. This chapter examines how NLP-enabled user-centric design makes the world more accessible and inclusive for those who deal with cross-border financial transactions.

Furthermore, NLP goes beyond exchanges between parties. It includes the capacity to draw insightful conclusions from unstructured data, including support requests, social media posts and consumer evaluations. With the use of this feature, remittance platforms may have a better knowledge of user demands by being able to comprehend user feelings, preferences and pain concerns. This section's discussion traces how natural language processing (NLP) converts transactional exchanges between users into meaningful and dynamic discussions, setting the stage for a more tailored and intuitive user experience.

Sentiment analysis shows up as a useful adjunct to user interaction on remittance systems. Real-time sentiment analysis of users offers insightful information on customer happiness, issues and experiences in general. Through the examination of user-generated material, including reviews, comments and social media exchanges, remittance platforms are able to get a more comprehensive knowledge of user opinion. In addition to measuring user happiness, this section looks at how sentiment analysis may be used to proactively resolve problems, customise services and create an atmosphere that is more customer-focused and responsive.

Sentiment analysis is a critical tool for problem-solving and customer service. Remittance systems are able to recognise and rank issues that need to be addressed right away by keeping an eye on the emotion expressed in customer feedback and enquiries. By taking a proactive stance, platforms may respond quickly to issues and show that they value their users' contentment. Sentiment analysis also provides insights that are used to continuously enhance services, which helps to iteratively improve user experiences in the context of cross-border finance.

Sentiment analysis is also essential to user engagement and personalised marketing techniques. Remittance platforms may adjust marketing messaging, promotions and communication methods to better suit the emotions and preferences of their audience by comprehending the sentiments conveyed by users. Beyond transactional features, this degree of personalisation fosters a more comprehensive and interesting interaction between users and remittance services. This section delves into the ways that sentiment analysis serves as a catalyst for data-driven customer interaction initiatives that are also sensitive to the emotional context of consumers.

Although there are many advantages to integrating NLP and sentiment analysis, it's important to recognise and manage the difficulties these technologies provide when used to remittances. The subtleties of real language provide one of the main obstacles. Multilingualism, regional accents and slang vocabulary make it difficult to understand user input correctly. This chapter explores the methods used to deal with linguistic variety, such as the creation of multilingual models and ongoing training to improve language comprehension skills.

When handling user-generated content for sentiment analysis, privacy concerns also become more important. The ethical frameworks and procedures put in place to guarantee the appropriate management of user data, protect user privacy and extract insightful information are examined in this section. The conversation delves deeper into the challenging balancing act of extracting sentiment data for service enhancement while upholding user privacy rights in the dynamic context of data protection laws.

This section lays the groundwork for speculating on the future course of these technologies as it explains the nuances of sentiment analysis and natural language processing in remittance platforms. Sentiment analysis and natural language processing are dynamic fields that are always evolving as their full potential is explored. The future looks to further refine and sophistication, from the inclusion of sophisticated machine learning models for more precise language interpretation to the investigation of real-time sentiment data for instantaneous user involvement.

New avenues for innovation in user interactions are opened by the convergence of NLP and sentiment analysis with cutting-edge technologies like voice recognition and emotion detection. In order to provide consumers conducting cross-border transactions with more organic and intuitive conversational experiences, this section examines the possible synergies between natural language processing (NLP) and voice-enabled interfaces. Additionally, the investigation of emotion recognition technology gives insights into how remittance systems might evaluate user feelings to adjust services and support interactions accordingly. Furthermore, the trajectory for the future explores the function of natural language processing and sentiment analysis in light of changing user expectations and preferences. Remittance platforms can now anticipate user demands, preferences and attitudes because of enhanced personalisation methods. This means that interactions become more than just transactional; they become dynamic and responsive engagements. This chapter explores the prospects for designing a future in which cross-border financial transactions provide smooth, safe user experiences that are also sensitive to the emotional context of users.

Biometric Authentication and Fraud Prevention

The combination of artificial intelligence (AI) and Biometric Authentication for fraud prevention provides a strong barrier against fraudulent activities and unauthorised access in the ever-changing world of cross-border financial transactions. This section explores the significant effects of biometric authentication, including how remittances with biometric authentication improve security and how AI tactics strengthen fraud prevention protocols to protect international financial transfers.

One of the mainstays of remittance platform security is biometric authentication, which uses distinct biological characteristics to identify users. Passwords and PINs are examples of traditional authentication mechanisms that can be compromised by theft or unauthorised access. In order to mitigate these weaknesses, biometric authentication uses unique, innate biological traits—like voiceprints, iris patterns, fingerprints or facial features—to verify users.

User access and transaction initiation are transformed by the use of biometric authentication in remittances. This section examines how biometric modalities may be seamlessly integrated into remittance systems to provide a safe and convenient environment. A quick scan or detection of their distinct biometric markers can start transactions, provide access to account details and carry out a number of other tasks for users. Biometrics-based multifactor authentication strengthens security while streamlining the user experience, making cross-border finance more user-friendly and efficient.

Furthermore, this segment's topic threads across the benefits of several biometric modalities. For example, fingerprint recognition gives a dependable and frequently used approach, while facial recognition offers the ease of non-contact verification. Several biometric modalities together improve security levels, making it harder for bad actors to get around authentication procedures. As consumers interact with remittance systems, biometric authentication transforms from a security feature into a vital component that makes safe, user-focused international financial transactions possible.

Even though biometric authentication is a strong barrier against unwanted access, fraud is a dynamic field that calls for ongoing attention to detail and flexible solutions. Artificial intelligence is a valuable tool for bolstering fraud protection tactics in remittance platforms because of its ability to analyse data in real time, identify patterns and make proactive decisions.

The AI techniques used to identify and stop fraud in international financial transactions are covered in detail in this section. As a subset of artificial intelligence, machine learning algorithms are essential for sifting through large amounts of information in order to spot irregularities, spot trends that point to fraud and adjust to new risks. This segment's investigation reveals how artificial intelligence (AI)-driven fraud prevention transcends rule-based systems and offers a flexible and adaptable barrier against con artists' ever-evolving strategies.

Transaction monitoring is a prominent use of AI in fraud prevention. To spot variations from typical activity, AI systems constantly examine transaction patterns, user behaviours and contextual data. Alerts for more inquiry are triggered by unusual transaction amounts, unusual locations or patterns that differ from the user's past behaviour. AI-driven fraud prevention is real-time, which guarantees that consumers are safe from new threats while simultaneously cutting down on reaction times.

Additionally, AI helps identify efforts at account takeover and identity theft. AI algorithms build comprehensive user profiles by examining a variety of data sources, such as biometric data, user behaviour and past transaction trends. Unusual access locations or abrupt alterations in transaction patterns are examples of deviations from pre-established profiles that lead to extra security precautions or difficulties with authentication. This proactive strategy ensures that fraudulent activity is intercepted before it may undermine the security of user accounts and transactions.

Additionally, the incorporation of AI in fraud protection extends to anomaly identification in user interactions. Artificial intelligence (AI) systems can detect trends indicating automated assaults, including bot-driven activity or account enumeration efforts, by examining how users interact with remittance platforms. This section's discussion threads through the various ways artificial intelligence (AI) is being used to combat fraud, building a multi-layered defence system that can adjust to the complexities of the global financial scene.

Although the combination of AI-driven fraud detection and biometric authentication provides strong security measures, it is crucial to address the issues these technologies raise in relation to remittances. For example, the privacy of biometric data must be taken into account. This section discusses how remittance platforms negotiate the ethical and regulatory implications of collecting, storing and processing biometric information. User biometric data is managed responsibly, balancing security and privacy, thanks to the use of encryption, safe storage practices and compliance with data protection laws.

Another difficulty is interoperability, particularly when it comes to biometric authentication. It is vital to make sure that biometric systems can function and integrate across a variety of devices and networks as consumers interact with remittance platforms throughout the world. This section explores the standards and protocols designed to promote interoperability and make cross-border transactions seamless and easy for people to complete.

Furthermore, AI-driven fraud protection algorithms must constantly change due to the dynamic nature of fraud. This section's discussion delves into the tactics used to combat the idea of adversarial assaults, in which scammers make deliberate efforts to fool AI algorithms. AI-driven fraud protection is becoming more resilient to changing threats because of techniques like enhanced anomaly detection systems, ensemble learning and model retraining.

This part lays the foundation for speculating on the future course of these technologies as it explains the nuances of AI-driven fraud prevention and biometric authentication in remittance systems. There are constant developments and attempts to reach their maximum potential on this dynamic voyage. The future holds further sophistication and refinement, from the development of AI algorithms with improved predictive skills to the integration of new biometric modalities.

This section's investigation reveals the possible uses of cutting-edge biometric modalities such as behavioural biometrics, gait analysis and vein recognition. These modalities add extra security and uniqueness levels, making multifactor authentication systems stronger. Furthermore, the incorporation of continuous authentication offers a proactive safeguard against identity theft and unauthorised access by continually monitoring biometric data throughout user interactions.

The trajectory for the future also explores how AI might be used to build a fraud prevention environment that is more predictive and adaptable. Remittance systems are able to remain ahead of developing risks because of advanced machine learning models that are outfitted with real-time data streams and the capability to contextualise information. This section explores how proactive techniques, which anticipate and mitigate hazards before they affect consumers, replace reactive ones in AI-driven fraud prevention.

Furthermore, federated learning—a decentralised method of machine learning—has the potential to improve the security of AI-driven fraud prevention. This method creates a more secure and privacy-preserving environment by allowing models to be trained jointly across several devices without exchanging raw data. The upcoming course takes into account the advantages and possible uses of federated learning to build a more robust and private-aware fraud prevention environment.

To sum up, the investigation of AI-powered fraud prevention and biometric authentication in the context of remittance platforms is a voyage into the convergence of security and technology. A safe, reliable and user-focused global financial environment is made possible by these technologies, which redefine user authentication and provide adaptable fraud defence measures. In a future where security is not only a requirement but an assurance, biometric authentication and AI-driven fraud prevention become more than just security features as users interact with remittance platforms; they become defenders of user trust, strengthening the fundamentals of cross-border financial transactions.

Hyper-personalisation and Customer-Centric Services

The concept of hyper-personalisation and customer-centric services appears as a disruptive force in the ever-changing world of cross-border financial transactions, changing how people and companies interact with remittance platforms. In-depth discussion of hyper-personalisation's significant effects, its integration into remittance services and the transition to customer-centric AI solutions are covered in this part, which also highlights the significance of responsive and customised experiences in the international transfer of money.

Remittance services' hyper-personalisation marks a break from conventional one-size-fits-all strategies by recognising the various demands, interests and circumstances of users conducting cross-border transactions. This section examines the ways in which remittance platforms employ artificial intelligence (AI), data analytics and cutting-edge technology to customise services to the distinct needs and profiles of individual customers.

Customising user interfaces and experiences is a key component of hyper-personalisation. Remittance platforms employ artificial intelligence (AI) algorithms to examine user preferences, transaction histories and behaviours. Platforms can design user interfaces that suit individual tastes, straightforward navigation and personalised dashboards thanks to the knowledge gained from this investigation. This guarantees that customers can easily initiate and track transactions while also streamlining the user experience.

Hyper-personalisation goes beyond user interfaces to the level of service offers and suggestions. Remittance platforms may provide consumers customised recommendations, such as the best times to transfer money based on past exchange rate patterns, the most economical routes for transactions and customised offers or discounts, by utilising machine learning algorithms. This section explores how hyper-personalisation creates an environment where each encounter is tailored to the individual requirements and preferences of users, going beyond simple transactional efficiency.

Furthermore, communication channels are included in the personalisation integration of remittance services. Remittance platforms interact with consumers in real time by providing help, direction and customised insights using AI-driven chatbots and virtual assistants. In addition to answering questions about transactions, these chatbots often proactively offer details on industry trends, possible cost reductions and pertinent promotions. This section explores how hyper-personalisation in communication channels creates a more dynamic and personalised user experience by making the environment more responsive and interesting.

Remittance systems are being fundamentally reoriented with a focus on customer-centric AI solutions, which put the user at the centre of service design and delivery. This change underscores that AI technologies are not only instruments for improving procedures but enablers of a more inclusive, accessible and user-centric global financial environment.

This section explores the approaches and projects that remittance platforms have taken on to integrate a customer-centric mindset into their artificial intelligence solutions. The incorporation of user-driven insights and feedback loops is a crucial component of this change. Remittance systems employ AI to record and examine customer reviews, transaction trends and service quality ratings. Platforms may iteratively improve their AI models thanks to this real-time feedback loop, making sure that they always match changing consumer tastes and expectations.

Moreover, user empowerment is embraced by customer-centric AI systems. Giving people more power and transparency over their transactions is necessary to achieve this. AI algorithms are applied to evaluate transaction data and provide users with actionable information, such as the influence of exchange rate variations on transaction amounts or the projected time for fund transfers to reach their destination. This

44

section examines how the trend towards AI-enabled user empowerment gives consumers a sense of control and confidence, making the sometimes confusing world of cross-border banking easier to navigate.

This segment's investigation also goes into how AI might be used to design customised financial solutions that cater to the particular requirements of certain customer groups. Customer-centric AI solutions cater to a wide range of users, from individuals making modest remittances to family members to enterprises conducting large-scale cross-border transactions, and guarantee that the services provided meet the unique needs of each user. Predictive analytics integration makes it possible for platforms to foresee user demands and provide proactive solutions, which helps to create a more flexible and responsive global financial ecosystem.

Moreover, customer-centric AI solutions promote inclusion. This means creating AI models that accommodate users with different degrees of technological aptitude, linguistic preferences and financial knowledge. Remittance systems employ artificial intelligence (AI) to provide multilingual user interfaces, streamlined user manuals and instructional materials that enable users to make wise decisions. This section's topic covers how customer-centric AI solutions close the accessibility gap and guarantee that a wider range of users may profit from cross-border financial transactions.

While customer-centric AI solutions and hyper-personalisation have the potential to revolutionise the industry, it is critical to address the drawbacks of these strategies in the context of remittances. Using personal data ethically is one major difficulty. This section examines how remittance platforms strike a careful balance between user privacy and personalisation. An ethical and responsible approach to personalisation in remittance services involves the use of strong data protection mechanisms, compliance with privacy laws and open disclosure about data usage.

An additional problem to take into account is interoperability. It is imperative that remittance platforms be able to smoothly interface and communicate with a variety of financial networks and service providers as they progress towards more personalised and customer-centric models. This section explores the programmes and guidelines designed to promote interoperability and build a unified ecosystem that extends beyond the confines of certain remittance platforms.

In addition, the problem of bias in AI systems needs to be carefully considered. Biases that can unintentionally be present in the data or algorithms must be addressed since AI models have an impact on user experiences and service suggestions. This chapter delves into the ways that remittance platforms employ to mitigate prejudice and ensure fairness in AI-driven personalisation so as to prevent discriminatory consequences.

This section lays the groundwork for speculating on the future course of these technologies as it explains the nuances of hyper-personalisation and the move towards customer-centric AI solutions. There are constant developments and attempts to reach their maximum potential on this dynamic voyage. Future developments promise even more sophistication and refinement, from the incorporation of cutting-edge personalisation strategies to the development of AI models with improved user empathy.

This segment's investigation reveals the possible uses of cutting-edge personalisation methods like emotion-aware artificial intelligence. AI models are able to determine user emotions, stress levels and contentment by integrating emotional cues from user interactions. This allows platforms to customise services based on user emotional context in addition to transactional data. Furthermore, the incorporation of sophisticated AI-powered recommendation systems offers more perceptive and contextual suggestions, paving the way for a day when each user contact is customised and anticipatory.

The trajectory for the future also explores how AI may be used to address how consumer expectations in the cross-border financial sector are changing. More sophisticated machine learning models with natural language processing skills allow AI systems to understand user inquiries and reply more conversationally and contextually. This section's analysis reveals how customer-centric AI solutions will benefit from a conversation between customers and remittance systems that is relevant, responsive and tailored to each user's demands rather than merely improving transactional efficiency.

Furthermore, combining virtual reality (VR) and augmented reality (AR) technology has the potential to completely redefine the way users interact with remittance services. In order to create immersive and user-friendly interfaces where users can see and interact with their financial data in real time, this chapter examines the possible uses of AR and VR. These technologies' confluence with AI-driven personalisation brings up new possibilities for building a futuristic, user-focused and captivating global financial ecosystem.

CHAPTER 5

Enhancing Security and Compliance

The necessity of enhancing security and compliance is a cornerstone in maintaining the reliability, integrity and trustworthiness of international remittance platforms in the constantly changing world of cross-border financial transactions. The ever-present problem of protecting user assets, guaranteeing the security and integrity of sensitive information and abiding by a complicated web of regulatory regulations shapes the dynamics of remittance platforms. Not only are security and compliance operational aspects, but they are also the cornerstones upon which enterprises, regulatory agencies and user confidence are based. We dissect the technologies that strengthen the remittance platform architecture and provide strong defences against new threats, from sophisticated authentication techniques to cryptographic protocols.

Regulatory Compliance Through AI-Driven Analytics

AI-driven analytics for regulatory compliance is a revolutionary method of negotiating the complex world of international financial transactions. This creative synergy essentially uses artificial intelligence (AI) to improve

© Hari Prasad Josyula 2024
H. P. Josyula, *Redefining Cross-Border Financial Flows*,
https://doi.org/10.1007/979-8-8688-1064-0_5

the accuracy, speed and flexibility of compliance processes, making sure that financial platforms stay ahead of changing standards and comply with regulations.

By automating and streamlining numerous compliance activities, AI-driven analytics in regulatory compliance brings about a paradigm change. A type of artificial intelligence known as machine learning algorithms is used to examine large datasets and identify trends that could point to regulatory issues or anomalies. By taking a proactive stance, financial institutions and remittance platforms may quickly spot any compliance problems, reducing the chance of non-compliance and the dangers that come with it.

A noteworthy use of AI in regulatory compliance is the improvement of Know Your Customer (KYC) and Anti-Money Laundering (AML) procedures. The identification of suspicious activity, transaction tracking and identity verification of customers are all made easier by AI-driven analytics. AI models grow skilled at identifying abnormalities and possible compliance violations by continually learning from prior data and adjusting to developing trends. This strengthens the defence against illegal financial activity.

Furthermore, dynamic risk assessment is made possible by AI-driven analytics. AI offers a more dynamic and adaptable approach to compliance than traditional models, which frequently depend on static rules. To dynamically modify risk scores, machine learning models can assess transactional behaviour, contextual data and other pertinent aspects. This guarantees that compliance initiatives are both efficient and adaptable to the changing regulatory environment and the nature of financial transactions.

In the context of cross-border transactions, the integration of natural language processing (NLP) with AI-driven analytics further improves regulatory compliance. NLP makes it possible to analyse unstructured data, including news items, legal papers and regulatory texts. This allows for a thorough grasp of updates and changes to regulations. Financial organisations may use this capacity to remain up-to-date on changing legislation and modify their compliance practices accordingly.

Even while AI-driven analytics has the potential to revolutionise regulatory compliance, issues including ethical concerns, data privacy and model explainability still need to be properly addressed. Strong data security protocols, ethical standards and openness in AI decision-making processes are essential for fostering confidence and guaranteeing the ethical application of AI in regulatory compliance.

Importance of Regulatory Compliance

The value of regulatory compliance in cross-border financial transactions cannot be emphasised. As the global financial sector evolves, regulatory frameworks provide the foundation for trust, transparency and legality. This discussion delves into the multifaceted aspects that highlight the importance of regulatory compliance in the context of remittances, looking at how adhering to established standards not only protects the interests of various stakeholders but also ensures the integrity and stability of the broader financial system.

At its heart, regulatory compliance is critical to ensuring the financial stability of cross-border remittance networks. Financial institutions and remittance service providers are subject to a complicated web of restrictions aimed at preventing illicit activity such as money laundering, terrorism funding and other financial crimes. Compliance with strong Anti-Money Laundering (AML) and Counter-Terrorism Financing (CTF) rules is critical for reducing the risks connected with these illegal activities. Remittance platforms help to protect the global financial system from misuse and exploitation for illegal purposes by putting in place strong compliance requirements.

Regulatory compliance is critical in maintaining consumer trust and confidence in cross-border financial transactions. Users that use remittance platforms entrust them with sensitive financial information, and data protection standards guarantee that this information is handled responsibly and securely. The adoption of strong Know Your Customer (KYC) and Customer Due Diligence (CDD) processes not only meets legal requirements but also gives consumers trust that the remittance platform is dedicated to preserving their identities and financial assets. Because trust is the foundation of financial exchanges, regulatory compliance becomes critical to developing and sustaining solid connections between remittance platforms and their consumers.

The worldwide nature of cross-border transactions involves adherence to a plethora of international norms and standards. Different jurisdictions have different regulatory requirements, and navigating this complex terrain is a tough task for remittance systems. The necessity of regulatory compliance becomes clear when platforms strive to function smoothly across borders while conforming to the many legislative frameworks that regulate financial transactions. Successful compliance guarantees that remittance services are accessible to customers globally while following the particular restrictions imposed by each country, providing a standardised and integrated global financial network.

Noncompliance with regulatory norms exposes remittance platforms to legal and reputational problems, which can have serious implications. Entities that fail to comply with regulatory obligations may face penalties, sanctions or even revocation of their licences. Furthermore, legal consequences might ruin the brand of remittance platforms, resulting in a loss of user trust and confidence. The significance of regulatory compliance stems from its position as a shield against legal and reputational problems, offering a foundation for ethical and responsible behaviour in the cross-border financial landscape.

Regulatory compliance is a critical factor in maintaining the principles of financial inclusion and accessibility. By complying with rules that encourage fair and transparent financial services, remittance platforms help to democratise financial access. Compliance with consumer protection legislation guarantees that all users, regardless of financial knowledge or background, are treated fairly and equally. This adherence to regulatory requirements promotes an inclusive financial environment in which people from all socioeconomic levels may conduct cross-border transactions with confidence and security.

Contrary to popular belief, regulatory compliance may serve as a catalyst for responsible and long-term improvements in the financial technology industry. Regulatory frameworks create a controlled environment in which innovations can thrive while ensuring user interests and security are protected. Compliance constraints enable remittance platforms to implement cutting-edge technology like blockchain, artificial intelligence and biometric verification in ways that are consistent with established standards. This junction of innovation and regulation pulls the industry ahead, resulting in a scenario where technical innovations are used to improve user experiences while maintaining regulatory integrity.

Regulatory compliance is an effective instrument for resolving the issues created by financial crimes in the cross-border remittance industry. AML and CTF rules require remittance platforms to use comprehensive due diligence methods to detect and prevent questionable transactions. Compliant remittance platforms can detect and report potentially unlawful activity by scrutinising transaction patterns, conducting risk assessments and installing transaction monitoring systems. In this context, regulatory compliance is important because it serves as a proactive defence against financial crimes, contributing to the global effort to maintain the financial system's integrity.

Regulatory compliance entails not just conforming to domestic regulations but also promoting cross-border cooperation and collaboration. International regulatory agencies and efforts seek to provide a consistent regulatory framework across many jurisdictions. Compliance with these initiatives, such as the Financial Action Task Force (FATF) guidelines, allows remittance platforms to contribute to global efforts to combat financial crime and guarantee the safe and legal flow of cash across borders. This collaboration improves the efficacy of regulatory measures and supports a coordinated approach to ensuring the stability of the global financial system.

The regulatory landscape is always altering in response to new threats, technology breakthroughs and shifting geopolitical events. The relevance of regulatory compliance stems from remittance platforms' capacity to successfully respond to these changes. This necessitates ongoing monitoring of regulatory changes, proactive adjustments to compliance procedures and investments in technology that are compatible with changing requirements. Remittance platforms' adaptation to shifting regulatory climates supports their resilience and capacity to navigate the intricacies of the global financial sector.

AI-Driven Analytics for Ensuring Compliance

The capacity of AI-driven analytics to proactively detect and manage risks is one of its primary contributions to compliance. Conventional compliance techniques frequently rely on retroactive analysis and static regulations, which can cause reactions to new hazards to be delayed. This paradigm is altered by AI, which is driven by machine learning algorithms and continually analyses enormous datasets in real time. By taking a proactive stance, financial institutions and remittance platforms may spot any compliance problems early on and implement focused mitigation measures. Artificial intelligence (AI)-driven analytics serves as a watchful steward, enhancing the security and integrity of cross-border financial transactions by spotting irregularities in transaction patterns and potentially warning indications of fraud.

The regulatory environment that oversees financial transactions across borders is dynamic and always changing. When it comes to offering dynamic flexibility that complies with shifting regulatory standards, AI-driven analytics thrives. Financial institutions may remain up-to-date with the newest developments by using machine learning models that are taught to recognise and comprehend regulatory language. This feature guarantees that compliance procedures are both effective and adaptable to the subtle changes in legislation. AI-driven analytics makes it possible to seamlessly adapt to changing regulatory frameworks, reducing the chance of non-compliance and promoting an adaptable and robust compliance approach.

Know Your Customer (KYC) and Anti-Money Laundering (AML) procedures are crucial for banking industry regulatory compliance, and AI-driven analytics greatly improves them. The processes of client identity verification, transaction monitoring and suspicious activity identification are streamlined using machine learning algorithms. Large volumes of data, including past transaction patterns, may be analysed by these algorithms to find abnormalities that can point to possible fraud or money laundering. AI-driven analytics increases the effectiveness of AML and KYC while lowering the possibility of human mistake by automating these procedures. This strengthens the defence against illegal financial activity.

AI-driven analytics' real-time capabilities are essential for pattern detection and transaction monitoring. Conventional techniques sometimes entail batch processing and recurring assessments, which might cause delays in detecting questionable activity. Contrarily, artificial intelligence (AI) works in real time, continually analysing transaction data as it happens. This makes it possible to identify anomalous trends, transactions at high risk or departures from accepted standards quickly. Real-time transaction monitoring guarantees a proactive reaction to possible compliance issues, enabling interventions before any appreciable harm is done. Furthermore, AI's capacity for pattern recognition aids in the creation of increasingly complex models that are able to recognise subtle connections connected to a range of financial crimes.

Predictive analytics is where AI-driven analytics shines, giving financial organisations the capacity to foresee and get ready for upcoming compliance issues. Machine learning algorithms have the capability to forecast prospective areas of risk or impending regulatory needs through the analysis of previous data and trend identification. By planning ahead and staying ahead of regulatory changes, institutions may proactively improve their compliance practices and allocate resources more effectively. AI-enabled predictive analytics turns compliance from a reactive process into a proactive and strategic endeavour, putting financial platforms in a position to anticipate and respond quickly to the complexities of cross-border transactions.

One crucial component of compliance is regulatory reporting, which frequently requires a lot of human labour and has a high mistake rate. Regulatory reporting procedures are automated by AI-driven analytics, guaranteeing precision, effectiveness and compliance with reporting deadlines. Machine learning algorithms are capable of producing thorough reports, deciphering complicated regulatory requirements and extracting pertinent information from a variety of sources. Automation lessens the workload associated with manual operations and lowers the possibility of reporting mistakes. As a consequence, the regulatory reporting process is simplified and made more error-proof, which improves the overall effectiveness of compliance operations.

While there are many advantages to using AI-driven analytics to ensure compliance in international financial transactions, there are also issues and concerns that must be taken into account. Important aspects that require careful study are model explainability, ethical issues and data privacy issues. Building confidence with stakeholders and regulatory authorities requires making sure AI models are clear and easy to understand. Furthermore, the creation and application of AI-driven compliance solutions must take ethical factors like prejudice reduction and fairness into account. Sturdy data privacy safeguards that comply with international laws are essential for safeguarding private data and preserving user confidence.

In the context of compliance, AI-driven analytics must be transparent and comprehensible. Stakeholders and regulatory agencies want transparency in the decision-making process of AI models, particularly when such conclusions have a big impact on compliance. Explainability guarantees that financial organisations can effectively communicate with regulatory bodies by enabling them to explain and comprehend the rationale behind AI-driven compliance decisions. In addition to fostering confidence among stakeholders, transparent AI models support the appropriate and accountable application of AI in compliance operations.

The integration of AI-driven analytics into compliance procedures requires careful consideration of ethical issues. It is imperative to guarantee equity and minimise prejudices in artificial intelligence models, especially when working with a variety of datasets and user types. Financial institutions should put a high priority on ethical AI practices. They should thoroughly evaluate AI models to find and fix any biases that can affect compliance results. This dedication to moral issues promotes fairness in the treatment of users and stakeholders and builds confidence in the application of AI within legal frameworks.

Data is a key component of AI-driven analytics, and data protection is essential to upholding regulatory compliance. Strict data privacy requirements, including the General Data Protection Regulation (GDPR) and other legislation particular to certain jurisdictions, must be followed by financial institutions. Implementing comprehensive data encryption, anonymisation mechanisms and access restrictions guarantees that sensitive information is secured. Financial platforms that prioritise data protection when implementing AI-driven analytics not only adhere to legal requirements but also maintain consumer confidence.

Addressing Security Concerns in Cross-Border Transactions

Financial transactions involving many financial institutions, regulatory settings and technological platforms are inherently complex operations. The intricacy of the situation increases the likelihood of vulnerabilities and opportunities for malevolent actors to exploit it. Cross-border transactions raise a variety of security-related issues, from fraud and cyberthreats to geopolitical risks and regulatory compliance. In the digital age, financial institutions, IT companies, regulators and users all have a shared duty to solve these issues as financial transactions change.

The constant threat of cyberattacks is one of the main security issues in cross-border transactions. Cybercriminals are always looking for ways to take advantage of holes in digital infrastructure with the intention of breaking into financial systems without authorisation, stealing confidential information or interfering with transactions. Phishing scams, ransomware and Distributed Denial of Service (DDoS) assaults are examples of cyberthreats that may bring down financial networks. Financial institutions use strong cybersecurity measures, such as multi-factor authentication, intrusion detection systems and advanced encryption methods, to allay these worries and provide a strong barrier against online threats.

Cross-border transactions continue to be a source of constant worry due to fraud, as complex schemes can take advantage of weaknesses in verification procedures and transaction flows. Financial institutions use sophisticated fraud protection techniques, analysing transaction patterns, spotting abnormalities and identifying possibly fraudulent activity with the use of artificial intelligence (AI) and machine learning algorithms. In order to further reduce risk, enhanced Know Your Customer (KYC) protocols and biometric authentication verify the identity of consumers doing cross-border transactions. The security of financial transactions is maintained by prompt reactions to new fraud risks made possible by ongoing monitoring and real-time notifications.

One of the most important parts of handling security issues in cross-border transactions is regulatory compliance. Anti-Money Laundering (AML) regulations are essential for stopping illegal activity and guaranteeing the authenticity of cross-border fund transfers. Financial institutions use transaction monitoring systems, do due diligence on customers and follow strict KYC protocols in order to spot unusual activity that might be a sign of money laundering or terrorism funding. Adherence to international norms, including those established by the Financial Action Task Force (FATF), creates a structure that enhances the general safety and lucidity of financial transactions across borders.

Geopolitical considerations and regulatory dispersion among various nations impact cross-border transactions. There are extra complications and possible hazards because of the different legal systems and geopolitical environments. Financial institutions that do cross-border business must negotiate a variety of regulatory environments, some of which may differ in terms of financial reporting requirements, privacy rules and data protection legislation. Active interaction with regulatory agencies, adherence to global norms and the development of flexible compliance plans that take into account the unique characteristics of every jurisdiction are all necessary to mitigate these geopolitical risks.

Technology is a powerful instrument for addressing and mitigating risks in cross-border transactions, even as it also raises security issues. The strengthening of digital infrastructure is facilitated by ongoing developments in blockchain integration, secure application programming interfaces (APIs) and cybersecurity technologies. In particular, blockchain has become more well-known for its capacity to offer a visible and impervious record, lowering the possibility of fraudulent transactions. Secure APIs preserve data confidentiality and integrity while enabling easy communication between financial institutions. Security improvements are essential to keeping up with new threats and maintaining the stability of international financial institutions as technology advances.

Cross-border transaction security issues need cooperation between financial institutions, authorities and technology suppliers. The collective defence against security risks is strengthened by information exchange on compliance requirements, best practices and new threats. Establishing a network of trust and cooperation through cross-border collaboration allows stakeholders to work together to address issues and improve the security posture of the global financial ecosystem. The development of international standards, cooperative cybersecurity exercises and the exchange of threat intelligence are some of the initiatives that provide a robust and integrated defence against security threats.

Security problems are not limited to technology solutions and legal frameworks; they also include people. Cross-border transaction users are essential to the upkeep of security. Financial institutions spend money on user education and awareness campaigns to warn their clientele about the dangers of phishing, safe online conduct and the value of safeguarding private data. Improved cybersecurity literacy enables people to identify possible threats, take precautionary measures and add to the general safety of international financial transactions.

Cross-border transactions now provide both possibilities and concerns due to the advent of cryptocurrencies. Digital currencies present security threats, such as the possibility of money laundering, fraud and regulatory uncertainty, even while they have the ability to facilitate effective and borderless commerce. Financial institutions and authorities are keeping a close eye on and making adjustments to the changing bitcoin transaction scenario. Increased due diligence, digital asset-specific regulatory frameworks and cutting-edge blockchain-based solutions all help to reduce the dangers that are becoming more prevalent when using cryptocurrencies in cross-border financial transactions.

Cross-border transaction security issues highlight the significance of resilience and continuity planning. Strong business continuity and disaster recovery strategies are put in place by financial institutions to guarantee that crucial systems continue to operate even in the case of unanticipated circumstances or security incidents. The resilience of cross-border financial infrastructure is enhanced by frequent testing, scenario planning and the construction of redundant systems, which lessen the effect of any interruptions on transactional integrity.

Role of AI in Ensuring Security and Compliance

The potential of artificial intelligence to facilitate proactive threat identification and prevention is one of its main contributions to the field of security. Conventional security methods frequently depend on rule-based frameworks, which might not be able to adequately adjust to the ever-changing landscape of cyber threats. Financial institutions may now use AI, especially machine learning algorithms, to analyse large datasets and identify trends that could indicate security risks. AI models can detect abnormalities and possible threats in real time by continually learning from past data, which enables prompt responses before security breaches happen. The robustness of cross-border transactions against new dangers like malware, phishing assaults and other cyber threats is greatly increased by this proactive strategy.

The ability of AI to assess risk dynamically is essential for managing the complexity of cross-border transactions. Static risk models are typically used in the traditional approach; however, artificial intelligence brings a dynamic and adaptable technique. To dynamically modify risk scores, machine learning models can assess transactional behaviour, contextual data and other pertinent aspects. By doing this, it is made sure that risk assessments are correct and adaptable to the changing regulatory environment and the nature of financial transactions. Financial institutions may efficiently manage and reduce risks by using the flexibility of AI-driven risk assessment, which promotes a safe environment for cross-border financial activity.

Artificial intelligence (AI) has a revolutionary effect on Know Your Customer (KYC) and Anti-Money Laundering (AML) procedures, which are essential to regulatory compliance. Large-scale data analysis is a skill that machine learning algorithms possess, since they can quickly spot trends that might be signs of possible money laundering. These algorithms expedite transaction monitoring, identity verification for customers and the identification of questionable activity. Financial institutions may save human labour and ensure a more complete and accurate evaluation of the risks associated with cross-border transactions by automating and optimising AML and KYC procedures through the incorporation of AI. This improves compliance while also adding to the financial system's general integrity and security.

Real-time AI skills are essential for anomaly identification and transaction monitoring. Conventional techniques sometimes entail batch processing and recurring assessments, which might cause delays in detecting questionable activity. AI is a real-time system that continually analyses transaction data as it happens. This makes it possible to identify anomalous trends, transactions at high risk or departures from accepted standards quickly. Real-time transaction monitoring guarantees a proactive reaction to possible security and compliance issues, enabling interventions before any appreciable damage is done. The ability of AI to detect anomalies aids in the creation of more complex models that are able to recognise subtle patterns connected to a range of financial crimes.

The ability of AI to do predictive analytics is crucial in equipping financial institutions to tackle upcoming security threats. By evaluating past data and finding trends, machine learning models may forecast prospective areas of risk or upcoming security concerns. Institutions may proactively improve their security plans, distribute resources effectively and remain ahead of evolving cyber threats using this forward-looking strategy. By transforming security from a reactive procedure to a proactive and purposeful endeavour, predictive analytics enables financial platforms to move with agility and foresight through the intricacies of cross-border transactions.

A strong option for guaranteeing the security of cross-border transactions is AI-driven biometric authentication. AI algorithms are used by biometric technologies, like voice authentication, facial recognition and fingerprint recognition, to enable very accurate and safe identity verification. By confirming that people conducting financial transactions are who they say they are, biometric authentication improves security in cross-border transactions where user identities need to be thoroughly confirmed. By preserving the integrity of user identities throughout the transactional process, this helps to ensure regulatory compliance in addition to preventing unauthorised access.

One essential element of AI that makes cross-border regulatory compliance easier is natural language processing, or NLP. NLP algorithms are capable of deciphering and interpreting unstructured data, such as legal papers, compliance rules and regulatory texts. Financial institutions use natural language processing (NLP) to remain abreast of changing regulatory frameworks and make sure their compliance procedures adhere to the most recent guidelines. The capacity to evaluate and derive valuable insights from a variety of textual sources improves the effectiveness of compliance initiatives and adds to a thorough and current knowledge of regulatory requirements in different jurisdictions.

By automating compliance procedures, artificial intelligence (AI) greatly lessens the workload associated with human activities and improves the effectiveness of cross-border transactions. AI-driven solutions may automate routine compliance duties, including transaction monitoring, data verification and regulatory reporting. This reduces the possibility of human mistake while also quickening the compliance procedure. The use of automated compliance processes guarantees a methodical and uniform approach to meeting regulatory obligations, thus augmenting the general security and lucidity of financial transactions across borders.

AI makes it possible to create security architectures that are adaptable and can change to counter new threats. While AI-driven security systems are able to adapt and learn from new problems, traditional security solutions may find it difficult to keep up with the fast growth of cyber threats. Security procedures may be regularly updated by machine learning algorithms, which can also analyse data on newly discovered attack vectors. By being flexible, security measures are able to keep up with the most recent attacks, giving financial institutions a dynamic defence against the ever-changing cyber hazards associated with cross-border transactions.

Transparency and ethical issues become crucial as AI plays a major part in security and compliance. Financial institutions are responsible for ensuring that AI models function morally, devoid of prejudice and discriminatory tactics. It is crucial for AI models' decision-making processes to be transparent, particularly when such judgements have a big impact on security and compliance. Building confidence and encouraging responsible use of these technologies is achieved by open communication with stakeholders, including regulatory agencies, regarding the ethical standards and guiding principles driving AI-driven security measures.

CHAPTER 6

Impact on Financial Inclusion

AI-driven breakthroughs in cross-border transactions have a far-reaching influence on global financial inclusion, going beyond security and regulatory concerns. AI technologies are critical in breaking down old barriers, increasing accessibility and guaranteeing that a wider range of people can actively engage in the global financial system.

AI-powered technologies improve and simplify cross-border transactions, making financial services more accessible to people in underserved areas. Automation and digitalisation minimise dependency on traditional banking infrastructure, allowing consumers to conduct transactions via mobile devices and Internet platforms. This increased accessibility empowers people who may have limited access to brick-and-mortar financial institutions, promoting financial inclusion for those who were previously excluded from traditional banking services.

The use of AI in cross-border transactions helps to reduce transaction costs. Automation and process optimisation minimise inefficiencies, cutting total international money transfer costs. As a result, individuals, particularly those in economically challenged areas, benefit from lower-cost financial services. The reduced financial burden encourages more involvement in cross-border transactions, bridging the gap for groups that have previously been excluded due to high transaction costs.

© Hari Prasad Josyula 2024
H. P. Josyula, *Redefining Cross-Border Financial Flows,*
https://doi.org/10.1007/979-8-8688-1064-0_6

Breaking Down Barriers for the Unbanked

In the current global financial landscape, removing obstacles for the unbanked is an essential task. Developments in AI-driven technology are crucial in tackling the difficulties encountered by people who lack access to traditional banking services. This talk explores the various ways that artificial intelligence (AI) is promoting financial inclusion by removing obstacles and opening doors for the unbanked community.

Lack of access to standard banking services is one of the main obstacles facing the unbanked. Financial exclusion is exacerbated by physical remoteness, inadequate infrastructure and a shortage of physical financial institutions. AI-driven technologies, in particular digital financial platforms and mobile banking, have shown to be effective instruments for providing banking services to the unbanked. Through the use of AI algorithms, mobile banking applications make financial transactions safe, effective and easy to understand. This makes it possible for people in underserved areas to use their smartphones to access banking services. Geographical restrictions are removed by this digital revolution, enabling unbanked people to engage with the formal financial system.

Because they do not have access to official banking systems, a large number of unbanked persons rely on cash transactions. The unbanked are integrated into the digital financial ecosystem by means of AI-driven technologies that digitise cash transactions. AI-driven digital payment systems and mobile wallets enable microtransactions as well as peer-to-peer and bill-paying activities. These technologies lessen dependency on real currency by offering a safe and practical cash substitute, improving financial security and transparency for the unbanked.

Due to their frequent lack of collateral or credit history, the unbanked face major obstacles when trying to obtain credit. Artificial intelligence (AI)-powered lending platforms are revolutionising the microfinance industry by opening up modest loans to those who were previously shut out of traditional credit systems. To determine creditworthiness, machine learning algorithms examine a variety of different data sources, including transaction histories and mobile usage trends. With the help of this creative strategy, financial institutions may now provide microloans to the unbanked, encouraging small companies, entrepreneurship and economic development in previously underserved populations.

Conventional Know Your Customer (KYC) procedures can be laborious and demanding, necessitating a large amount of documentation that the unbanked might not have. This obstacle is addressed by AI-powered biometric authentication, which offers a quick and safe way to confirm someone's identification. Through the use of distinctive biological characteristics, biometric technologies—such as fingerprint, face and iris recognition—allow people to validate their identities. This guarantees a strong and safe verification procedure, even for those without conventional identity documents, and expedites the financial services onboarding process.

Lack of knowledge and comprehension of financial concepts can make it difficult for the unbanked to effectively participate in the formal financial system, which makes financial literacy another important obstacle. AI-powered systems provide individualised financial education based on each user's unique requirements and reading level. Through chatbots or mobile applications, machine learning algorithms examine user behaviours and preferences to provide relevant and easily assimilated financial information. By providing the unbanked with the information and abilities necessary to make wise choices about savings, investments and other financial endeavours, this individualised approach improves financial literacy.

The unbanked must have access to dependable customer service in order to develop confidence and trust. Artificial intelligence (AI)-powered chatbots and virtual assistants offer quick and easy customer service, answering questions and assisting customers with different financial procedures. The AI-driven help systems function round the clock, surmounting temporal and linguistic obstacles that may hinder correspondence through conventional customer care avenues. Artificial intelligence improves user experience and motivates unbanked people to keep using financial systems by making support services more accessible.

People are frequently hindered by worries about data security and privacy, especially in areas where identity theft and financial fraud have a history. AI is essential for bolstering the security of financial transactions and safeguarding user information. Advanced encryption techniques, anomaly detection systems and real-time monitoring help to create a safe environment for the unbanked to engage in digital financial operations without compromising their privacy. In order to encourage the unbanked to switch from traditional cash transactions to digital financial systems, it is imperative to establish confidence through strong security measures.

The unbanked population may find it difficult to utilise digital financial services due to language problems. Localised language support is made possible by AI-driven language processing technologies, which remove language barriers and guarantee that users may communicate with financial systems in their native tongue. This inclusiveness is essential to improving the usability and accessibility of digital financial instruments and serving the multilingual groups for whom traditional banking services might not be available.

In order to effectively reach the unbanked, partnerships and community involvement are made possible by AI. Financial institutions may identify target populations and customise their outreach initiatives with the use of predictive analytics and machine learning algorithms. Data-driven insights boost partnerships with community leaders, local organisations and non-governmental organisations (NGOs), allowing for a more focused and effective approach to financial inclusion programmes.

Financial institutions can keep an eye on socioeconomic shifts in their communities, modify their offerings and react to changing demands thanks to artificial intelligence's analytical powers. Understanding the financial behaviours of the unbanked is possible through the analysis of transactional data, spending trends and economic indicators by machine learning models. Financial inclusion initiatives stay current and adaptable to the changing requirements of the unbanked population thanks to the information provided in the creation of new financial products and services that take into account the changing socioeconomic landscape.

Case Studies on Expanding Financial Inclusion Through AI

Case studies on leveraging AI to increase financial inclusion offer concrete illustrations of how AI technologies are empowering people to access underprivileged markets, dismantling conventional obstacles and promoting economic emancipation. These examples demonstrate creative thinking, effective applications and the revolutionary potential of artificial intelligence in the field of financial inclusion.

Artificial intelligence-powered mobile banking services have become important drivers of financial inclusion in a number of Sub-Saharan African nations. One noteworthy instance is M-Pesa in Kenya. Using AI-driven technology, M-Pesa, which is Swahili for 'Mobile Money', enables users to do a variety of financial transactions using their mobile phones. The platform enables users to send and receive money, pay bills and obtain microloans—even if they don't have typical bank accounts. In order to evaluate creditworthiness, AI algorithms examine user behaviour and transaction patterns. This makes it easier to provide financial services to a group of people who were not previously banked. The success of M-Pesa shows how geographical boundaries may be broken down and people in underserved and distant areas can access critical financial services thanks to AI-driven mobile banking.

An innovative example of using AI-powered biometric authentication to improve financial inclusion is the Aadhaar system in India. Identity verification is made safe and effective with Aadhaar, a unique identifying system based on biometric information like fingerprints and iris scans. The unbanked people may now create bank accounts, apply for government subsidies and conduct digital financial transactions thanks to the system's integration with other financial services. In addition to streamlining the onboarding process, AI-driven biometric authentication solves the issue of inadequate documentation, which is a frequent barrier for the unbanked. Aadhaar is an example of how biometric technology may significantly increase financial inclusion when it is incorporated into financial institutions.

Artificial intelligence is being used in Latin America to rethink credit rating systems, especially for those without a traditional credit history. Brazilian financial technology startup Nubank has used AI algorithms to evaluate credit risk and extend credit cards to those who would not have been eligible for regular banking services. To assess creditworthiness, the AI-powered credit scoring system examines data from a variety of sources, such as utility bills and behavioural trends. Due to Nubank's creative strategy, financial services are now available to a larger portion of the populace, promoting financial inclusion in an area where many have previously had difficulty obtaining credit.

In order to encourage financial inclusion in Southeast Asia, blockchain technology—a type of artificial intelligence—has been used. One example is the blockchain-based Everex platform, which enables financial services and cross-border transactions. Everex evaluates credit risk using AI algorithms before providing microloans to locals. The integration of blockchain technology into the platform guarantees safe, transparent and economical transactions, hence mitigating the drawbacks of conventional banking systems. This study highlights how the confluence of blockchain and AI may produce novel solutions to solve financial inclusion concerns, especially in locations with complex regulatory regimes and limited access to traditional banking infrastructure.

AI-driven chatbots have been used in South Asia, especially in Bangladesh and Pakistan, to provide the unbanked people with individualised financial education. These chatbots converse with customers in their native tongues while offering advice on savings techniques, fundamental financial ideas and the advantages of traditional banking. They are driven by natural language processing (NLP) algorithms. These chatbots are important tools for improving financial literacy and enabling people to make wise financial decisions since they customise material to the unique requirements and literacy levels of their users. This example shows how targeted education programmes using AI may close the knowledge gap and advance financial inclusion.

Artificial intelligence (AI)-driven systems for remote digital identity verification have been used in the Middle East to support financial inclusion. Governments and financial organisations in the area have embraced technology that verifies people's identities virtually without requiring them to be there, using facial recognition and AI algorithms. This strategy has made financial services more accessible to the unbanked, expedited account opening procedures and decreased the need for traditional documents. The instance illustrates how AI-powered identity verification improves the onboarding process speed, which is essential for accessing marginalised communities.

Sub-Saharan African agricultural populations encounter particular difficulties in obtaining banking services. AI algorithms are used by organisations like Hello Tractor and other AI-driven agricultural finance projects to evaluate smallholder farmers' creditworthiness. To assess the risk of granting loans, these algorithms examine past crop yields, weather trends and agricultural data. Financing institutions may provide farmers with customised financing packages that allow them to purchase inputs such as seeds and equipment by utilising AI in this way. This instance demonstrates how AI meets the unique requirements of farming communities, promoting greater financial inclusion in rural areas.

In Southeast Asia, artificial intelligence (AI)-powered solutions have advanced microinsurance, a crucial aspect of financial inclusion. Businesses such as BIMA use AI algorithms to evaluate risk, personalise insurance policies and streamline the claims procedure for those who have little access to conventional insurance services. AI in microinsurance not only makes operations run more smoothly, but it also makes it possible to customise insurance plans to meet the specific requirements of the unbanked population. This example shows how AI can make insurance more accessible to everyone by giving those who weren't previously eligible for it financial security.

CHAPTER 7

AI and Cryptocurrencies in Remittances

Artificial intelligence (AI) is essential for streamlining remittance operations in a number of ways. To estimate transaction flows and optimise currency exchanges, AI-powered prediction models examine past transaction data, user behaviour and market trends. Users may send money across borders more quickly and affordably thanks to this predictive capacity, which also helps to lower transaction costs and improve the effectiveness of remittance services.

Cryptocurrencies, such as Bitcoin and Ethereum, run on decentralised blockchain technology. Transparency, security and transaction immutability are guaranteed by this system. Blockchain reduces the possibility of fraud and improves the general security of remittance transfers by making it easier to create a decentralised ledger that logs every transaction.

AI and cryptocurrency work together to provide quick and affordable remittance transfers. AI systems make the best choice of cryptocurrencies according to the state of the market, guaranteeing that customers get

© Hari Prasad Josyula 2024
H. P. Josyula, *Redefining Cross-Border Financial Flows*,
https://doi.org/10.1007/979-8-8688-1064-0_7

good exchange rates. Because cryptocurrencies are decentralised, they do not require middlemen, which lowers transaction costs and speeds up the transfer process. As a consequence, those sending and receiving remittances have a more streamlined and economical experience.

Blockchain Technology in Remittances

Blockchain technology has been a disruptive force in the remittance industry, changing the way cross-border transactions are often conducted. The transparent and decentralised technology that powers cryptocurrencies like Bitcoin has several benefits for remittance businesses. This conversation explores the various uses, advantages, difficulties and long-term effects of using blockchain technology in the international remittance system.

The fundamental idea behind blockchain technology is decentralisation, which is the process by which a dispersed network of nodes keeps an agreement on the current state of a shared ledger. This decentralisation removes the requirement for a central authority, like a bank, to supervise and verify transactions in the context of remittances. Transparency and immutability are guaranteed as each member of the blockchain network maintains a copy of the ledger. This feature reduces the possibility of fraud in addition to improving security because each transaction is logged and confirmed by several network nodes.

The idea of smart contracts—self-executing contracts with the contents of the agreement explicitly put into code—is introduced by blockchain technology. Smart contracts can automate many parts of the transaction process in remittances. For instance, the smart contract can automatically carry out the following actions when specific predetermined criteria are satisfied, such as the successful completion of a financial transfer. This automation speeds up transactions and lessens reliance on middlemen, enabling cross-border transfers that are both quicker and more affordable.

The expenses of remittance transfers are greatly decreased by blockchain's decentralised structure. Conventional approaches frequently entail a number of middlemen who bill for their services. Blockchain streamlines the process and lowers transaction costs by doing away with the need for these middlemen. The blockchain network may have low fees for users, which makes it an affordable option for people and companies who send money back and forth.

The strong security properties of blockchain make it the perfect answer to remittance security issues. The use of cryptographic algorithms assures the integrity and secrecy of transaction data. A transaction is practically impervious to tampering once it is registered on the blockchain, lowering the possibility of fraudulent activity. The blockchain ledger's visible and auditable characteristics provide prompt identification of any inconsistencies, hence augmenting the overall security of cross-border transactions.

Traditional remittance methods frequently have delays because of things like time zone variations, banking hours and processing times for intermediaries. Real-time settlements made possible by blockchain technology enable immediate cross-border transfers. For people whose financial requirements depend on timely remittances, this function is very helpful. Furthermore, because blockchain technology is decentralised, transactions may take place around-the-clock, giving customers uninterrupted access to remittance services without being limited by regular banking hours.

Blockchain technology has the potential to promote global financial inclusion by providing access to financial services to those who lack or have limited access to banking services. Users can conduct cross-border transactions using blockchain-based remittance systems without requiring a conventional bank account. Blockchain's accessibility supports initiatives to bring underprivileged groups into the official financial system by enabling them to send and receive money anywhere in the world.

Even while blockchain technology has clear advantages for remittances, there are still obstacles and restrictions. One major obstacle is scalability. The scalability of a blockchain system becomes increasingly important as the volume of transactions on the network rises. Scaling problems plague a lot of the current blockchain networks, which causes delays and higher transaction costs when demand is strong. For blockchain to be widely used in the high-volume context of international remittances, scaling issues must be resolved.

The regulatory environment pertaining to cryptocurrencies and blockchain technology is still developing, and adhering to current financial standards might be difficult. For blockchain-based remittance services to be legitimate and accepted by the larger financial ecosystem, they must comply with know your customer (KYC) and Anti-Money Laundering (AML) rules. The lack of established legislation internationally adds difficulty to the deployment of blockchain in remittances, necessitating coordination between industry players and regulatory agencies to set clear norms.

The integration of blockchain technology with the current financial infrastructure presents challenges. A lot of financial organisations are still using outdated technology, which can make it difficult for them to integrate blockchain networks. Bridging the gap between traditional banking systems and blockchain technology needs large investments in infrastructure upgrades and concerted efforts among financial institutions to assure compatibility.

Because blockchain technology is still in its infancy, user adoption and education present substantial obstacles. People who are used to using traditional remittance methods can be reluctant to adopt blockchain-based alternatives because they don't know enough about them or don't trust them. To get past this obstacle and promote broad adoption, education campaigns emphasising the advantages, security features and usability of blockchain remittance systems are crucial.

Future advances are laid down by the use of blockchain technology into remittances. With the advancement of technology, resolution of scalability concerns and modification of legislative frameworks, blockchain holds promise as the foundation of a decentralised and mutually compatible worldwide financial system. With the emergence of stablecoins and central bank digital currencies (CBDCs) significantly boosting the effectiveness of blockchain-based transfers, cross-border transactions may go beyond conventional fiat currencies.

AI Integration with Cryptocurrencies for Seamless Transactions

A ground-breaking advancement, the fusion of AI with cryptocurrencies offers a synergistic approach that improves the effectiveness, security and user experience of financial transactions. This dynamic combination of artificial intelligence (AI) and cryptocurrencies offers a paradigm shift in the way that transactions are carried out, guaranteeing smooth operations, sophisticated analytics and increased security.

Among the most common uses of AI in relation to cryptocurrencies is the creation of automated trading systems. In order to find patterns and forecast future price movements, artificial intelligence (AI) algorithms, in particular machine learning models, examine enormous datasets, market trends and past price movements. By enabling automated trading bots to execute buy or sell orders on customers' behalf, these predictive analytics enable real-time trading strategy optimisation. This not only removes the requirement for ongoing human oversight but also permits quick trade execution based on complex AI-driven insights.

Artificial intelligence (AI)-powered technologies improve market analysis in the cryptocurrency arena by offering thorough insights into market dynamics. To determine the sentiment of the market, natural language processing (NLP) algorithms examine textual data such as news articles, social media posts and other texts. Because traders and investors may evaluate the general sentiment of the market as well as possible price fluctuations, sentiment analysis helps them make well-informed judgements. Large-scale unstructured data may be processed and interpreted by AI, which helps with rapid and accurate market evaluations that impact trading choices in the erratic cryptocurrency markets.

The use of AI in cryptocurrency extends to the administration of dynamic portfolios. To suggest the best asset allocations, AI algorithms examine users' investment portfolios, risk tolerance and market circumstances. These suggestions adjust in real time in response to shifts in the financial landscape and market conditions, making sure that customers' portfolios remain diverse and well-balanced. With AI's capacity to continually learn from market data and modify strategies to optimise returns while controlling risk, this dynamic approach to portfolio management is made possible.

Cryptocurrencies are vulnerable to fraud because of their decentralised and pseudonymous nature. Artificial intelligence (AI) technology, namely, machine learning models, is essential for identifying and stopping fraud in bitcoin transactions. These algorithms look for abnormalities suggestive of fraudulent activity by analysing network activity, user behaviour and transaction patterns. AI can adjust its fraud detection algorithms by continually learning from fresh data, offering a strong defence against changing cyberthreats in the bitcoin ecosystem.

The bitcoin transaction user experience is improved via AI-driven personalisation. Platforms that integrate AI technology may adapt interfaces, alerts and suggestions based on users' preferences, behaviour and transaction history. In addition to streamlining the user experience, this personalised approach increases trust and user engagement. The capacity of AI to comprehend personal preferences helps create a bitcoin transaction environment that is more user-friendly and intuitive.

Artificial intelligence (AI) has been extended to trading platforms using natural language processing (NLP). Users can communicate with trading platforms by utilising natural language instructions since NLP algorithms are able to interpret and comprehend human language. As a result, the trading process is made simpler and more approachable for a wider range of users, including those with no technical experience. NLP-driven interfaces enable users to conduct trades, check account balances and get market information using easy and conversational interactions.

Artificial intelligence (AI)-powered predictive analytics is essential for predicting changes in cryptocurrency prices and market patterns. To forecast future price changes, artificial intelligence (AI) systems use historical data, technical indications and outside variables. These forecasts help traders and investors manage risks, take advantage of opportunities and make data-driven choices. Predictive analytics produced by AI helps consumers manage the naturally turbulent nature of cryptocurrency markets by promoting a more knowledgeable and strategic approach to bitcoin transactions.

The combination of AI and cryptocurrency allows for sophisticated risk control and flexible trading methods. In order to dynamically modify trading tactics, machine learning algorithms evaluate risk variables, market volatility and consumers' risk tolerance. With the help of this adaptive strategy, users may react instantly to shifting market conditions, reducing risk and optimising profits. Users are better equipped to manoeuvre the intricacies of cryptocurrency markets with dexterity and accuracy because of AI's ongoing learning and adaptability.

The banking industry's difficulties with regulatory compliance are addressed by the combination of AI and cryptocurrency. AI algorithms analyse transaction patterns, spot suspicious activity and guarantee regulatory compliance, all of which help bitcoin platforms adopt strong Anti-Money Laundering (AML) procedures. When combined with AI-driven compliance solutions, the transparency and traceability provided by blockchain technology create a more compliant and safe environment for bitcoin transactions.

The combination of AI with cryptocurrency has many benefits, but there are drawbacks as well as moral dilemmas. Because AI-driven trading is automated, there are worries about market manipulation and the possibility that algorithmic trading would increase volatility in the market. Furthermore, biases in training data and model outputs must be carefully taken into account when using AI for predictive analytics. It is imperative to guarantee equity, lucidity and responsibility in AI-facilitated cryptocurrency dealings in order to tackle ethical issues and foster confidence within the wider financial system.

The combination of artificial intelligence and cryptocurrency is a developing industry with lots of room for growth. Advances in decentralised finance (DeFi), quantum computing and reinforcement learning might further change the cryptocurrency transaction environment as technology develops. The efficiency and inclusiveness of cryptocurrency ecosystems might be improved by innovations like AI-powered decentralised exchanges (DEXs) and decentralised autonomous organisations (DAOs).

CHAPTER 8

Overcoming Ethical and Social Challenges

The combination of blockchain, cryptocurrencies and artificial intelligence has created previously unheard-of chances for innovation and change in the quickly evolving fields of finance and technology. This chapter offers a balanced viewpoint while recognising the enormous potential for good transformation. It emphasises the necessity of making ethical decisions and taking responsibility for them in order to shape the future of technology. It acts as a catalyst for stakeholders from a range of sectors, such as business, academia and policymaking organisations, to work together to negotiate the ethical terrain of the digital era.

Ethical Considerations in AI Algorithms

As artificial intelligence (AI) becomes more and more integrated into our daily lives, revolutionary shifts occur along with a range of ethical questions. Of these, the ethical aspects of AI algorithms are particularly important and need close examination. Examining the ethical issues raised by algorithms' development, use and social effect is crucial as these tools become more and more integrated into decision-making processes across industries, from banking and employment to healthcare and criminal justice.

© Hari Prasad Josyula 2024
H. P. Josyula, *Redefining Cross-Border Financial Flows,*
https://doi.org/10.1007/979-8-8688-1064-0_8

The problem of bias is one of the main ethical issues with AI systems. Because algorithms learn from past data, a biassed set of historical data might cause an AI system to reinforce preexisting social biases. For instance, in recruiting algorithms, the AI model can unintentionally reproduce gender or racial prejudices if previous hiring data reflects them. This might result in biassed outcomes. In order to guarantee just and equal treatment for people from a variety of demographic backgrounds, ethical considerations need a concentrated effort to detect and reduce biases in AI systems.

AI algorithms' lack of explainability and transparency presents moral dilemmas about user trust and responsibility. Deep neural networks are among the many sophisticated AI models that function as 'black boxes', making it difficult to comprehend how they make certain judgements. Algorithm opacity becomes a major ethical challenge in crucial fields where judgements affect people's lives, such as healthcare and finance. To foster trust and guarantee that consumers are able to understand, inquire about and contest algorithmic judgements, it is imperative to strike a balance between the intricacy of AI models and the requirement for openness.

Large volumes of data are crucial for the training and decision-making of AI algorithms. Concerning the privacy of the people whose data is exploited, ethical issues arise. Privacy rights may be violated by the gathering, storing and use of personal data for AI applications like predictive policing or targeted advertising. In order to minimise possible disadvantages related to the exploitation of sensitive information, it is vital that ethical considerations be made to safeguard persons' privacy and set clear norms for responsible data usage.

An intricate ethical conundrum arises when deciding who is responsible when AI algorithms make choices. When an artificial intelligence (AI) system makes a bad choice that has unfavourable effects, assigning blame is complicated. Clarity on who should be held responsible for algorithmic mistakes or biases is required by ethical considerations. To guarantee responsible AI development and deployment, a balance must be struck between the autonomy of AI systems and the accountability of those creating, deploying and supervising them.

If inclusion is not considered throughout the design process, AI algorithms may unintentionally reinforce systemic inequality. Concerns regarding discriminatory effects are raised when facial recognition algorithms, for example, show reduced accuracy rates for particular demographic groups. Ethical issues underscore the necessity of testing AI technology across a variety of datasets and people in order to prevent the reinforcement or amplification of pre-existing societal imbalances.

Widespread AI implementation might change labour markets and result in job displacement in some industries. Beyond technical issues, ethical considerations in AI algorithms also take the effects of automation into account. Navigating the shift to an AI-driven future in a way that prioritises reskilling the workforce, reduces economic inequality and promotes a fair and reasonable distribution of the advantages obtained from AI developments is ethically vital.

A further ethical concern is striking the correct balance between algorithmic autonomy and human control. 'Human-in-the-loop' artificial intelligence models underscore the significance of human supervision and involvement, particularly in pivotal decision-making situations. Ethical AI deployment requires finding a balance between utilising AI's efficiency and making sure that human judgement is not compromised.

To mitigate algorithmic bias, mitigation strategies must be put into practice. Adoption of methods like fairness-aware machine learning, in which models are specifically created to account for and reduce biases, is encouraged by ethical considerations. The integration of varied viewpoints during the development process, continuous monitoring for biases and routine audits of algorithms are crucial measures in guaranteeing that AI systems enhance social values.

Because AI applications are global in scope, ethical questions need to go beyond national borders. Global norms and governance frameworks must be established in order to guarantee that AI algorithms always follow moral guidelines. Working together, governments, industry players and regulatory agencies may forge a unified moral framework that directs the ethical advancement and application of AI technology.

Ethics also play a role in raising awareness and educating people about AI technology. Making sure that developers, decision-makers and the general public are aware of the ethical ramifications of AI algorithms is crucial. Programmes for AI education that incorporate ethical issues can enable people to advocate for ethical AI activities and make well-informed judgements.

Strategies to Mitigate Bias in Remittance Platforms

A fundamental strategy to mitigate bias in remittance platforms is to prioritise data diversity and representation. Biases often arise from historical data that may reflect existing inequalities. By diversifying the dataset used for training AI models within remittance platforms, developers can ensure a more comprehensive representation of demographics, regions and transaction patterns. This approach helps prevent the perpetuation of pre-existing biases and enhances the platform's ability to cater to a wide range of users fairly.

Implementing algorithmic fairness frameworks is instrumental in mitigating bias. These frameworks involve incorporating principles and metrics that explicitly address fairness concerns. For remittance platforms, this could mean designing algorithms that prioritise equal treatment across user demographics, irrespective of factors such as nationality or income level. Fairness-aware machine learning models can be employed to continuously assess and adjust algorithms to align with predefined fairness criteria.

Regular audits and bias monitoring are essential components of a comprehensive strategy to mitigate bias in remittance platforms. Periodic assessments of the platform's algorithms and decision-making processes help identify and rectify biases as they emerge. This proactive approach ensures that any unintended biases are promptly addressed, fostering an environment of continuous improvement and fairness within the remittance platform.

Ensuring transparency and explainability in the decision-making processes of remittance platforms is a crucial strategy to mitigate bias. Users should have a clear understanding of how decisions, such as fee calculations or transaction approvals, are made. Transparent algorithms enable users to scrutinise the platform's operations, which not only builds trust but also empowers users to identify and report instances of bias, contributing to a collaborative effort to ensure fairness.

A user-centric design philosophy can significantly contribute to mitigating bias in remittance platforms. By prioritising accessibility and inclusivity, developers can create platforms that cater to diverse user needs. This involves considering factors such as language preferences, user interfaces suitable for various demographics and ensuring that the platform is accessible to individuals with varying levels of technological literacy. An inclusive design approach minimises the risk of unintentional biases that may arise from overlooking the diverse needs of the user base.

Establishing ethical guidelines and providing training for developers are foundational elements in the mitigation of bias in remittance platforms. Developers should be educated on the ethical considerations surrounding bias and equipped with tools and methodologies to identify and address biases during the development lifecycle. Ethical guidelines serve as a compass, guiding developers to make decisions that prioritise fairness and ethical considerations in the design and deployment of remittance platforms.

Engaging with the user community and establishing feedback mechanisms are vital strategies to mitigate bias. Users from diverse backgrounds may provide valuable insights into potential biases that developers might overlook. By fostering a community-driven approach, remittance platforms can tap into the collective knowledge of their user base, identify bias concerns and collaboratively work towards solutions. This inclusive approach ensures that the platform evolves with user needs and remains responsive to emerging fairness challenges.

Adhering to regulatory compliance and incorporating external oversight are crucial strategies in the mitigation of bias in remittance platforms. Regulatory bodies can set standards and guidelines to ensure fairness and non-discrimination in financial services. External oversight, such as audits conducted by third-party organisations, adds an extra layer of scrutiny, validating that the platform operates in accordance with ethical and legal standards. This dual approach reinforces a commitment to fairness and bolsters user trust in the remittance platform.

To mitigate bias effectively, remittance platforms should adopt localised decision-making processes that account for cultural nuances and regional disparities. Decision-making algorithms should be sensitive to the cultural context of users, avoiding decisions that may inadvertently favour or disadvantage specific cultural or regional groups. This localised approach contributes to a more personalised and equitable experience for users across diverse geographical and cultural backgrounds.

Educating users about the potential biases in remittance platforms and raising awareness about fair financial practices is an impactful strategy. Informing users about their rights, the factors influencing transaction fees and the platform's commitment to mitigating bias fosters an informed user base. Education campaigns can also empower users to recognise and report instances of bias, promoting a collaborative effort to maintain fairness within the remittance platform.

Social Impacts of AI-Driven Financial Systems

The potential for improved financial inclusion and accessibility is one of the benefits AI-driven financial systems may have for society. AI makes it possible to create cutting-edge financial services and solutions that benefit those who were previously underserved or shut out of traditional banking systems. Financial firms may reach a wider audience and provide banking, loans and investment options by utilising AI algorithms to evaluate creditworthiness and expedite approval procedures.

The societal effects of AI-powered financial systems are not without difficulties, though. The possibility of discrimination and algorithmic prejudice are two major causes for concern. When educated on skewed datasets, AI systems have the potential to reinforce and magnify current societal injustices. This might show up in the financial sector as discriminatory practices or biassed loan choices that disproportionately impact marginalised populations. It is vital to overcome algorithmic bias to guarantee that AI-driven financial systems contribute to equal access and opportunity for all.

Concerns over job displacement and economic inequality arise from the possibility for the broad use of AI in financial systems to change the nature of employment markets. The need for particular employment may decline as a result of the automation of basic financial operations like data entry and customer support, which would affect people who hold those positions. While AI-driven systems lead to new job prospects in fields such as AI research and maintenance, proactive steps like social safety nets and upskilling programmes are needed to mitigate possible negative effects on vulnerable people.

Positively, financial systems powered by AI can personalise their interactions with customers. Large volumes of data are analysed by these systems in order to comprehend personal preferences, habits and financial requirements. Customised financial services, individualised advice and a more user-centric strategy are the final results. As a result, customers have a better overall experience, and they also feel more empowered since they have greater influence over their financial decisions.

AI-powered financial systems have societal repercussions that go beyond worries about data security and privacy. Because these systems are dependent on large-scale data gathering and analysis, it becomes critical to protect people's private financial information. Unauthorised access and data breaches have the potential to damage public confidence in AI-powered financial services. To solve these issues and preserve users' right to privacy, it is imperative to establish strong data protection mechanisms, encryption methods and clear data usage regulations.

AI-driven financial systems bring ethical issues concerning decision-making processes and accountability. As algorithms take judgements on their own that affect people's financial lives, concerns about the moral principles behind these decisions surface. To address the ethical issues and foster confidence in AI-driven financial systems, it is imperative to establish transparent algorithmic decision-making practices, defined ethical rules and accountability mechanisms.

Financial literacy and the digital divide are two other societal issues that are impacted by AI-driven financial systems. Even while these systems provide cutting-edge financial services, people with poor digital literacy or no access to technology may fall behind. Enhancing financial literacy and making AI-driven financial products accessible and intelligible for a wide variety of users are essential to closing the digital divide.

Changes in market dynamics and possible systemic concerns are brought about by the integration of AI in financial systems. For instance, high-frequency trading algorithms have the potential to impact market swings and provide difficulties for established market players. Maintaining the stability and integrity of financial markets depends on comprehending and reducing the systemic risks connected to AI-driven financial operations.

The societal effects of AI-driven financial systems demand comprehensive regulatory frameworks and governance mechanisms. Keeping up with technology improvements is a problem for policymakers who must make sure that rules change to meet new dangers and issues. In the field of AI-driven finance, a proactive regulatory strategy is necessary to find a balance between promoting innovation and defending social interests.

The effective integration of AI-driven financial systems into society depends on consumer trust. Transparency, unambiguous information about the advantages and disadvantages of AI and a dedication to moral behaviour are necessary for establishing and preserving confidence. For AI-driven financial technology to be widely used and have good social acceptability, security, privacy and fairness problems must be addressed.

CHAPTER 9

AI-Powered Market Insights and Global Remittance Trends

Global remittance patterns are being completely transformed by AI-powered market insights, which provide previously unheard-of possibilities for research, forecasting and optimisation in the cross-border financial sector. Financial institutions and remittance service providers are now able to extract relevant insights from large datasets through the integration of artificial intelligence (AI) into market research and analysis. This allows for more strategic planning and well-informed decision-making.

The capacity to identify and predict trends is one of the main benefits of AI-powered market insights in the field of international remittances. With the help of machine learning capabilities, artificial intelligence (AI) algorithms can forecast future trends by analysing market dynamics, economic indicators, historical remittance data and geopolitical factors. Through proactive responses to shifting market conditions, legislative changes and economic volatility, stakeholders may optimise their remittance plans thanks to this predictive potential.

© Hari Prasad Josyula 2024
H. P. Josyula, *Redefining Cross-Border Financial Flows*,
https://doi.org/10.1007/979-8-8688-1064-0_9

AI-Powered Market Insights

A revolutionary moment has arrived in the fields of corporate intelligence and strategic decision-making with the introduction of AI-powered market insights. With its unmatched ability to extract valuable insights from large and complicated datasets, artificial intelligence (AI) is transforming the way businesses analyse and understand data. AI-powered solutions are increasingly essential for market analysis, giving companies a competitive edge through real-time analysis, trend forecasting and data-driven decision-making. This thorough investigation explores the many facets of AI-powered market insights, looking at their importance, uses and consequences for many businesses.

AI-powered market insights are significant because they can process, analyse and extract useful information from large databases at rates and scales that are not possible for humans. Conventional market analysis frequently struggled to manage massive amounts of both structured and unstructured data. These databases include patterns, correlations and trends that AI systems, powered by machine learning and deep learning approaches, are excellent at spotting, providing a detailed insight into market dynamics. This improved analytical capability enables organisations to manage obstacles in a dynamic and linked global context, take advantage of new possibilities and make well-informed decisions.

Predictive analytics is one of the more notable uses of AI in market insights. Organisations may predict future market movements by using AI algorithms that can analyse previous data to find patterns and trends. AI-powered predictive analytics is especially useful for sectors like banking, where precise and timely forecasts of market movements may impact investment choices, maximise portfolios and reduce risks. Organisations may improve their strategic stance in the market by using machine learning models to obtain a forward-looking viewpoint.

In an ever-changing industry, the ability of AI-powered market analytics to provide real-time insights is essential. Artificial intelligence (AI) algorithms have the ability to process and analyse data in real time, giving businesses the most recent information on consumer trends, market situations and competitive environments. This flexibility is essential for quick decision-making, allowing companies to quickly adjust to shifting conditions, seize momentous opportunities and tackle new problems. Since customer patterns may change quickly in sectors like e-commerce, real-time market monitoring is very helpful.

Understanding customer behaviour and preferences is largely dependent on market insights driven by artificial intelligence. AI systems may find patterns that provide deep insights into customer preferences by examining enormous datasets that include customer interactions, purchase histories and Internet behaviours. Businesses are able to improve the entire consumer experience, customise marketing campaigns and personalise their offers thanks to this information. Artificial intelligence (AI)-driven insights into consumer behaviour are reshaping the landscape of customer-centric company strategies, from recommendation engines in e-commerce to personalised content distribution in media.

AI-powered market insights are a major asset in industries like banking and cybersecurity where risk management is critical in recognising possible threats and spotting fraudulent activity. Algorithms using machine learning techniques can examine past data to find unusual trends that can point to fraud. This results in stronger fraud detection systems in financial institutions, protecting against harmful activity and guaranteeing transaction security. The proactive aspect of AI in risk management strengthens the resilience of businesses against unanticipated difficulties.

One of the main components of modern business intelligence is the incorporation of AI-powered market insights into strategic decision-making procedures. Decision-makers may assess market trends, competitor actions and upcoming opportunities holistically with the help of these insights. Organisations may better allocate resources, position themselves strategically within their sectors and match their aims with market realities by integrating AI-driven data into their strategic planning. As a result, negotiating the complexity of a cutthroat corporate climate may be done in a more flexible and resilient manner.

Although market insights enabled by AI have many benefits, there are drawbacks and moral dilemmas to be aware of. It is necessary to address problems like algorithmic bias, data privacy and the possibility of unforeseen effects in order to ensure the ethical use of AI. If algorithmic bias is not properly addressed, it might exacerbate already-existing disparities and lead to distorted perceptions and decisions. The responsible management of sensitive data, accountability for the results of AI-driven choices and openness in algorithmic processes are all examples of ethical issues.

Applications for AI-powered market insights may be found in a variety of sectors, each of which uses these skills to take advantage of particular opportunities and difficulties. AI analytics can evaluate patient data in the healthcare industry to forecast illness outbreaks and allocate resources as efficiently as possible. AI-powered predictive maintenance in manufacturing ensures maximum efficiency by foreseeing equipment faults. AI is used in the retail industry for customised marketing campaigns, inventory optimisation and demand forecasting. Applications of AI are flexible, making them a useful tool for businesses looking for data-driven answers to difficult problems.

Future developments in AI-powered market insights appear to be promising in terms of ongoing innovation and improvement. Organisations will be able to extract insights from textual data, such as social media and consumer reviews, thanks to advancements in natural language processing (NLP) and sentiment analysis. This will provide them a more thorough grasp of market sentiment. By combining AI with other cutting-edge technologies like blockchain and the Internet of Things (IoT), market insights will become even more comprehensive, providing a comprehensive picture of linked ecosystems.

Global Remittance Trends

The world of cross-border financial transactions has changed significantly in recent years due to substantial shifts in global remittance trends. The money that international workers send home to support their families is known as remittances, and it has long been a vital component of global economies and lifestyles. In this investigation, we explore the complex aspects of global remittance patterns, looking at the variables affecting their development, the influence of technology breakthroughs and the worldwide economic and social ramifications.

In many underdeveloped countries throughout history, remittances have been a vital source of economic assistance for families. In order to sustain their families and boost local economies, migrant labourers frequently go to economically developed regions in search of employment opportunities. In areas like South Asia, Latin America and Sub-Saharan Africa that mostly depend on the revenue from migrant workers, the importance of remittances to the economy is especially noticeable. Families depend on remittances to pay for everyday necessities like healthcare, education and housing.

Over time, a variety of variables have altered the dynamics of global remittances. Remittance patterns are erratic due to a variety of factors, including changes in immigration laws, geopolitical events, currency exchange rates and economic situations in both the home and host nations. The amount and flow of remittances are heavily influenced by the state of the world economy, which is marked by swings in income and job prospects.

The introduction of new technologies and the broad use of digital platforms is one of the radical factors influencing changes in international remittances. Digital alternatives to traditional remittance routes, which are sometimes associated with expensive transaction fees and protracted processing delays, are becoming more and more prevalent. The use of mobile money, Internet platforms and fintech solutions has become commonplace as a convenient and economical way for people to send and receive money across borders.

Improving financial inclusion has seen a radical shift with the emergence of mobile remittance services. Through the use of straightforward, easily available mobile devices, mobile money platforms allow people without access to traditional banking services to send, receive and manage monies. This has enormous consequences for communities in rural or disadvantaged places, providing them with financial skills and connection. The combination of technology and remittances works well together to support the overarching objective of promoting financial inclusion worldwide.

The amalgamation of cryptocurrency with blockchain technology signifies a further frontier in the transformation of worldwide remittance patterns. A less expensive and quicker method of transmitting money across borders is offered by cryptocurrencies like Ethereum and Bitcoin. The decentralised and transparent ledger system of blockchain technology improves the security and traceability of remittance transactions. The emergence of cryptocurrencies as a disruptive factor in the remittance industry is due to their ability to ease currency conversion difficulties and expedite international money transfers.

Positive developments are brought about by technological advancements, yet conventional remittance methods continue to confront obstacles. Exorbitant transaction expenses, sometimes linked to fees levied by financial intermediaries, continue to be a noteworthy worry. Prolonged processing periods can cause delays in the timely transmission of cash, especially in areas with intricate regulatory environments. Issues with currency exchange, wherein changes in exchange rates affect the recipient's ultimate amount received, add to the difficulties encountered by conventional remittance routes.

Geopolitical upheavals and economic changes have an impact on global remittance trends. Remittance trends and volume have been impacted by economic downturns like the COVID-19 epidemic and the global financial crisis of 2008. During such situations, limits on movement, border closures and changes in work prospects might upset the customary patterns of remittance transfers. Global remittance patterns are dynamic in nature, partly due to currency fluctuations, immigration policy changes and geopolitical conflicts.

Remittances have a significant impact on recipient nations' economies in addition to their direct effects on individual households. Remittance inflows support investments in regional companies, better access to healthcare and education and higher household spending. Remittances can act as a stabilising factor in some situations, giving families in areas where migrant labour is widely relied upon a steady stream of income during economic downturns.

Examining global remittance trends from social and environmental angles is becoming more common. The environmental effect of cross-border financial transactions is being reevaluated due to the carbon footprint connected with traditional remittance systems, especially with regard to travel to physical remittance facilities. The adoption of socially responsible remittance practices, such as financial literacy campaigns and community development projects, is growing in popularity as stakeholders become more aware of the wider obligations that come with remittance flows.

A combination of elements, such as continuous technical breakthroughs, geopolitical changes and alterations in economic paradigms, will influence the future trajectory of global remittance patterns. The remittance environment is expected to undergo additional transformation due to the ongoing digitisation of financial services, the incorporation of blockchain technology and the possible widespread acceptance of cryptocurrencies. The way that remittances develop in the upcoming years will be greatly influenced by regulatory frameworks, global partnerships and advancements in financial infrastructure.

CHAPTER 10

Future Trends and Predictions

Global remittances are expected to undergo a paradigm shift in the future, driven by new patterns and projections that represent the changing dynamics of cross-border financial transactions. A noteworthy development is the combination of cryptocurrencies with blockchain technology, which provides safe and decentralised substitutes for established remittance networks. Blockchain's transparent ledger technology boosts security, decreases transaction costs and streamlines the transfer process, while cryptocurrencies like Bitcoin and Ethereum provide prospects for speedier and cost-effective cross-border transactions.

Remittances are expected to become increasingly digital in the future, with a rising inclination towards Internet and mobile platforms. It is anticipated that fintech solutions and digital wallets will offer people an easy-to-use and effective way to transfer and receive money internationally. This move to digital platforms is consistent with the larger pattern of technology improvements reshaping the financial services industry.

Remittance platforms are expected to see an increase in the use of artificial intelligence (AI), especially when it comes to risk management and fraud prevention. The security of cross-border financial transactions will be improved by AI algorithms' capacity to examine transaction

H. P. Josyula, *Redefining Cross-Border Financial Flows*,
https://doi.org/10.1007/979-8-8688-1064-0_10

patterns and identify abnormalities. Users' confidence is fostered by the proactive integration of AI-driven analytics, which guarantees the security and integrity of the remittance ecosystem.

Emerging Technologies in Cross-Border Finance

Emerging technologies and their integration are bringing about a fundamental revolution in the cross-border financial scene. In addition to changing the way that financial procedures are done, these technologies are bringing in previously unheard-of levels of efficiency, security and potential for international trade. This investigation explores the most important new technologies in cross-border finance, looking at their uses, implications and potential to change the landscape of global financial transactions in the future.

Blockchain technology is leading the way in the transformation in cross-border banking. The decentralised and distributed ledger technology known as blockchain makes it possible to securely and openly record transactions involving several participants. Blockchain eliminates the need for middlemen in cross-border financing, cutting costs and processing times. Smart contracts, which are self-executing agreements with their terms encoded straight into code, enable automated and trustless transactions, thus simplifying international financial transactions. Global financial transaction practices are changing dramatically as a result of blockchain's potential uses in trade finance, remittances and cross-border payments.

With the help of the trailblazing example of Bitcoin, cryptocurrencies have become a decentralised kind of international digital money. Peer-to-peer transactions are made possible by these digital assets, which do not require traditional banking institutions or middlemen. The use of cryptocurrencies in international finance offers a cost-effective and global substitute for conventional fiat currencies. Because cryptocurrencies are decentralised, they improve financial inclusion by enabling people to engage in the global economy even if they do not have access to traditional banking services. The integration of cryptocurrencies into cross-border financial institutions is growing as the legal environment changes.

A major advancement in the digitalisation of national currencies is represented by the idea of Central Bank Digital Currencies, or CBDCs. Digital copies of a nation's official currency, issued and managed by its central bank, are known as CBDCs. The goal of these virtual currencies is to bring together the benefits of blockchain technology with the security and government control of fiat money. The implementation of collateralised debt certificates (CBDCs) in international finance has the capacity to optimise transactions, augment financial inclusion and bestow increased authority over monetary policy on central banks.

Technologies like artificial intelligence and machine learning are essential to optimising several facets of cross-border banking. AI-driven applications are improving accuracy and efficiency in a variety of fields, including fraud detection, risk assessment, customer service and data analysis. Artificial intelligence (AI) algorithms are able to analyse large datasets, spot trends and find abnormalities in know-your-customer (KYC) and Anti-Money Laundering (AML) operations. This results in increased security and regulatory compliance. Additionally, when new data becomes available, machine learning models may adjust and develop, enhancing their capacity for prediction in domains like market movements and currency exchange rates.

Software robots, or 'bots', are used in robotic process automation (RPA) to automate repetitive and rule-based processes. RPA is simplifying procedures like data input, transaction verification and reconciliation in cross-border finance. RPA lowers the possibility of mistakes, improves operational effectiveness and frees up human resources for more difficult and strategic duties by automating repetitive processes. Using RPA in cross-border finance is helping to improve overall operational agility and expedite transaction processing.

By linking tangible items to the digital world, the Internet of Things (IoT) is establishing a network that allows objects to share data and communicate with one another. IoT has applications in trade finance and supply chain finance in cross-border finance. IoT-enabled smart devices may deliver up-to-date information on the whereabouts, state and progress of cargo in real time. Data transparency lowers the risk of fraud, improves supply chain financing efficiency and empowers stakeholders to make better decisions based on up-to-date information.

The future of computer power is represented by quantum computing. The encryption methods used in international banking may change as a result of quantum computing's capacity to process enormous volumes of data tenfold more quickly than traditional computers. Although quantum computing might be a danger to existing encryption techniques, it also presents a chance to create cryptographic systems that are more safe. To guarantee the ongoing security of financial transactions in the quantum age, there is intensive research being done in the field of cross-border banking and the integration of quantum-resistant encryption techniques.

Strong cybersecurity measures are essential as digital technologies play a bigger role in cross-border banking. Sensitive financial information must be protected by using multi-factor authentication, strong encryption and the built-in security capabilities of blockchain technology. Cybersecurity technology is always changing to combat new threats and make sure that cross-border financial systems are secure from hackers and unauthorised access.

A crucial component of cross-border banking is regulatory compliance, and RegTech solutions are starting to appear to make compliance procedures more efficient. The RegTech toolbox includes blockchain-based audits, AI-powered analytics and automated reporting systems. By facilitating the more effective navigation of intricate regulatory environments, these technologies help financial institutions maintain compliance with global norms and reduce the risk of non-compliance.

The integration of developing technologies is changing cross-border finance by opening up previously unheard-of security measures, efficiency and opportunities for international trade. The decentralised ledger of blockchain technology and the global reach of cryptocurrencies are two examples of the developments that are causing a paradigm change in the way that financial transactions are carried out internationally. The potential for transformation is further enhanced by the convergence of AI, IoT and quantum computing, which combine to create a technologically sophisticated and dynamic environment for cross-border financial activities. With these technologies developing and blending together, a more integrated, effective and inclusive global financial system is anticipated in the future of cross-border finance.

Predictions for the Future of Remittances with AI Technology

An improved user experience is one of the main forecasts for the usage of AI in remittances in the future. Applications powered by AI are anticipated to streamline and customise the complete remittance process, from start to finish. Users will be able to communicate with remittance systems in a more conversational and user-friendly way thanks to natural language processing (NLP) technologies. AI-powered chatbots and virtual assistants will aid consumers with transactions by answering questions and offering real-time support. The goal of this improved user experience is to increase remittance accessibility for a wider range of people, especially those with low levels of technology literacy.

AI technology has the potential to streamline the many phases of money transfer procedures. Sophisticated prediction models will be essential in predicting exchange rates so that consumers may select the best times to transfer money. The time it takes for funds to reach recipients will be shortened by streamlining transaction processes through automation powered by AI-driven algorithms. Robotic Process Automation (RPA) will reduce mistakes and improve overall operational efficiency when used in transaction verification and processing. Remittance transactions should become quicker, more dependable and more affordable as a result of these optimisations.

Remittance services will be able to provide hyper-personalisation thanks to AI technology's capacity to analyse large datasets. In order to provide individualised suggestions and services, AI algorithms may evaluate the behaviour, preferences and transaction history of the user. This might involve specific recommendations for the best times to move money, preferred methods for exchanging currencies and even individual financial counselling. The goal of hyper-personalisation is to provide a more engaging and customer-focused remittance experience by meeting each user's specific demands.

The future of remittances must address security issues, and artificial intelligence (AI) is predicted to be a key component in preventing fraud. AI-powered biometric authentication will improve remittance transaction security. To lower the possibility of fraudulent activity, users' identities will be verified through the use of biometric identifiers such as fingerprint scans and facial recognition. The remittance ecosystem will gain an extra layer of protection as machine learning algorithms continually examine transaction patterns to spot irregularities and possible fraud cases.

Predictions regarding the future of remittances stress the significance of AI-driven analytics in maintaining regulatory compliance. AI will play a key role in negotiating and adjusting to shifting compliance requirements as the regulatory landscape changes. Real-time transaction monitoring and analysis by AI algorithms can identify any violations from regulatory norms. By taking a proactive approach to compliance, remittance service providers may lower their exposure to legal problems and penalties while ensuring that their transactions comply with global regulatory standards.

AI-powered market insights will play a major role in the future of remittances. We will analyse global trends, economic data and currency movements using machine learning and predictive analytics. Remittance platforms will be able to provide consumers with insightful market information thanks to this foresight, enabling them to make well-informed decisions regarding their transactions. Remittance flow predictions will become more accurate with the use of AI-driven market data, enabling service providers to adjust to shifting market conditions.

One audacious forecast for remittances in the future is the shift towards independent financial transactions. Blockchain technology combined with AI is anticipated to allow smart contracts to autonomously carry out and settle transactions according to predetermined criteria. This degree of automation might speed up the entire transfer process, minimise transaction costs and drastically decrease the need for middlemen. Autonomous financial transactions are in line with the larger trend of decentralised finance (DeFi) and anticipate an automated, trustless future for financial transactions.

The incorporation of AI technology is projected to significantly push the usage of cryptocurrencies in cross-border payments. Stablecoins and other cryptocurrencies provide an alternative, quicker and less expensive way to move money across the world. AI systems are capable of analysing user preferences and market situations to enable the best bitcoin transfers. By combining AI with cryptocurrencies, consumers will have more options and freedom when it comes to sending and receiving money, which will put existing banking channels to the test.

CHAPTER 11

Recommendations and Strategies

Remittance companies stand to gain a great deal from the application of artificial intelligence (AI) in terms of increased client satisfaction, increased efficiency and increased competitiveness in the constantly changing financial sector. In order for remittance services to fully reap the benefits of AI, companies need to take strategic measures that are in line with their goals and the evolving demands of their clientele.

Creating a clear roadmap for the deployment of AI is an important first step. A thorough evaluation of current procedures, the identification of problem areas and the formulation of doable objectives for AI integration should all be part of this plan. A staged strategy reduces interruptions to existing activities and guarantees a smooth integration process.

Optimising currency exchange rates and transaction processing times requires the use of sophisticated predictive models. Through the use of AI-driven predictive analytics, organisations may anticipate currency swings by gaining insights from past data, market patterns and user behaviour. This increases the overall effectiveness of remittance operations and enables them to provide rates that are competitive.

It is critical for organisations to address security concerns, and they may do so by using AI-powered fraud protection solutions. These systems use machine learning algorithms to identify and stop fraudulent activity

© Hari Prasad Josyula 2024
H. P. Josyula, *Redefining Cross-Border Financial Flows*,
https://doi.org/10.1007/979-8-8688-1064-0_11

in real time. Users feel more confident when financial transactions are secure because biometric identification, anomaly detection and pattern recognition are all integrated.

Businesses may utilise natural language processing (NLP) to make remittance transactions more straightforward and user-friendly. Users can get real-time information, assistance with transaction queries and guidance during the remittance process from chatbots or virtual assistants that are powered by natural language processing. This promotes a pleasant relationship between the consumer and the remittance platform and increases customer engagement.

AI-driven hyper-personalisation must be put into practice in order to customise remittance services to each user's preferences. Businesses may provide tailored recommendations, such as preferred transfer times, pertinent promotions and currency conversion possibilities, by examining user behaviour and transaction history. Customer happiness and loyalty are strengthened by this tailored experience.

Navigating the complicated environment of regulatory compliance is eased with the introduction of AI-driven analytics into remittance services. Algorithms constantly check transactions to make sure they adhere to global laws, Anti-Money Laundering (AML) regulations and Know Your Customer (KYC) guidelines. Taking proactive measures to resolve regulatory issues guarantees compliance with the law and fosters user trust.

Investing in AI-powered market insights makes it easier to stay ahead of industry trends and the dynamics of international remittances. By analysing economic statistics, market situations and user behaviour, machine learning algorithms give organisations insightful information that helps them make strategic decisions. By using a data-driven strategy, businesses can adjust to shifting market conditions.

One important tactic is to encourage collaboration and interoperability across borders. Collaborating with other financial institutions, fintech startups and payment service providers provides for interoperability across different remittance systems. By working together, remittance providers can reach a wider audience and give customers more choices when it comes to making foreign transactions.

For enterprises, another route to explore is the possibility of autonomous financial transactions. Blockchain technology with AI integration makes it possible to employ smart contracts, which automate and carry out transactions in accordance with preset criteria. This fits with the larger trend of decentralised finance (DeFi) by decreasing the reliance on middlemen and streamlining the entire remittance process.

When companies use AI into remittance services, ethical issues and transparency must come first. It is crucial to guarantee that AI algorithms are devoid of prejudices and that strict privacy regulations are followed while using personal data. Building trust and adhering to ethical standards are facilitated by open and honest communication with users on the function and implications of AI in remittance services.

Recommendations for Governments and Regulatory Bodies

Governments and regulatory agencies play a crucial role in developing rules that manage the integration of emerging technologies, including artificial intelligence (AI), in the constantly changing remittance services market. A number of important proposals can help governments create a legal framework that encourages innovation and guarantees the security, transparency and equity of cross-border financial transactions, therefore helping to successfully manage the potential and difficulties posed by AI in remittance.

A climate of proactive regulation is necessary. To comprehend the implications of artificial intelligence (AI) in remittance services, governments should actively engage with industry stakeholders and remain up-to-date on technical breakthroughs. Regulatory frameworks that combine promoting innovation with defending consumer interests and financial stability can be developed via cooperative efforts among regulatory agencies, financial institutions and technology specialists.

Clearly defining the rules for using AI is essential to provide companies a clear knowledge of their responsibilities. Regulatory agencies ought to address matters like data privacy, security protocols, algorithm openness in AI and moral issues. Users' trust in AI-driven remittance services is increased when there are clear regulatory frameworks in place, which provide a safe and reliable environment.

As AI grows more and more ingrained in remittance services, security issues become crucial. The monitoring and resolution of security-related concerns must be a top priority for governments. To protect the integrity of cross-border financial transactions, strong cybersecurity standards, frequent audits and adherence to international security norms are essential.

Another important suggestion is to promote innovation in regulatory compliance. Governments ought to provide incentives for the use of AI-powered regulatory technology (RegTech) solutions. These solutions contribute to a more effective and flexible regulatory system by streamlining compliance procedures, improving transparency and guaranteeing conformity to changing regulatory standards.

Because remittance services are international in nature, it is imperative that regulatory agencies collaborate across borders. A harmonised regulatory environment may be ensured by addressing issues with money laundering, fraud prevention and the smooth transfer of funds across borders through the standardisation of regulatory measures and the promotion of international collaboration.

Initiatives aimed at promoting financial inclusion must have active backing, especially in areas where traditional banking services are scarce. To promote equitable growth and broader economic development, governments should provide incentives for the use of artificial intelligence (AI) and other cutting-edge technology to provide financial services to the unbanked population.

Regulatory agencies have an obligation to handle the ethical and societal ramifications of artificial intelligence in remittance services. Building public trust and confidence in AI-driven financial systems is facilitated by regulations that guarantee impartial and fair AI algorithms, safeguard user privacy and minimise possible social repercussions.

Regulatory frameworks must be updated on a regular basis in order to stay up-to-date with technological changes. Governments must pledge to conduct regular evaluations, taking into account suggestions from business participants and adjusting to the rapidly changing international norms. When it comes to keeping regulations current and functional in the face of swift technological advancement, a dynamic regulatory approach guarantees this.

An important component of good governance is raising public awareness and education. Governments ought to fund public education initiatives to enlighten the public about the advantages and drawbacks of artificial intelligence (AI) in remittance services. Improving consumer knowledge of emerging technologies and financial literacy will enable them to make more informed choices and help the financial industry responsibly integrate artificial intelligence.

CHAPTER 12

Conclusion

This examination of altering remittances using AI technology demonstrates that the incorporation of artificial intelligence has enormous potential to revolutionise the landscape of cross-border financial transactions. Throughout the chapters, a thorough examination of various aspects of AI applications in remittances has revealed the potential of increased efficiency, security and personalised services. The confluence of sophisticated predictive models, blockchain integration, natural language processing and other AI-driven technologies envisions a future in which remittance services are not only more efficient but also more inclusive and customer-centric.

The journey through the obstacles of traditional cross-border transactions, such as high transaction prices, long processing times, currency exchange barriers and accessibility constraints, has highlighted the need for transformation. AI emerges as a catalyst for tackling these difficulties and opening up new opportunities for individuals and enterprises involved in global financial flows. The multidimensional approach, which includes security, compliance and user experience, demonstrates the entire impact AI may have on the remittance ecosystem.

Summary of Key Findings

The summary of major results from the investigation on reforming remittances with AI technology indicates a landscape brimming with disruptive possibilities. At the heart of these discoveries is the awareness

© Hari Prasad Josyula 2024
H. P. Josyula, *Redefining Cross-Border Financial Flows*,
https://doi.org/10.1007/979-8-8688-1064-0_12

that artificial intelligence (AI) is a potent force capable of fundamentally changing cross-border financial transactions. The combination of advanced predictive models, blockchain integration, natural language processing and other AI-driven technologies points to a future in which remittance services are not only more efficient but also more sensitive to the different demands of consumers.

One noteworthy result is the use of sophisticated prediction models, which allow for the optimisation of currency exchange rates and transaction processing times. This optimisation, powered by AI analytics, holds the potential for cost-effective and efficient cross-border transactions, solving long-standing issues associated with high transaction costs and long processing times in traditional remittance systems.

Blockchain integration appears as a vital component for maintaining transaction security and transparency. The summary emphasises that blockchain, together with AI, offers a viable answer to issues about fraud and trust in cross-border financial transactions. Blockchain technology's decentralised and tamper-resistant nature helps to build a secure platform for remittance services.

Another major result is the use of AI in promoting hyper-personalisation and customer-centric services. AI-driven systems may give personalised suggestions based on user behaviour and transaction history, providing consumers with a more customised and engaging experience. This not only improves client happiness but also demonstrates a trend towards more inclusive and user-friendly remittance operations.

The summary emphasises the need for regulatory compliance using AI-driven insights. This conclusion emphasises the proactive role of AI in managing the complex regulatory landscape of cross-border financial transactions. AI enhances security and legal compliance by continually monitoring transactions for conformity with international legislation, Anti-Money Laundering (AML) rules and Know Your Customer (KYC) standards.

AI-powered market insights have emerged as a key tool for analysing global trends. Machine learning algorithms can analyse market situations, economic indicators and user behaviours, providing data-driven insights to organisations and users. This not only helps with strategic decision-making but also prepares players to respond to changing market conditions, resulting in a more informed and dynamic financial ecosystem.

The report finishes with a forward-looking view on the evolution of autonomous financial transactions. This requires the integration of AI and blockchain technology, opening the path for decentralised and automated financial systems. The envisioned future includes a paradigm shift in which transactions are conducted smoothly based on predetermined circumstances, removing the need for middlemen and expediting the whole remittance process.

Encouraging the Adoption of AI in Remittances

Encouraging the use of artificial intelligence (AI) in remittances involves a diverse strategy that includes stakeholder participation, awareness-raising campaigns and strategic investments. At the heart of this endeavour is the awareness that effective integration of AI technology into remittance services is more than a technological improvement; it is a strategic requirement to fulfil the changing demands of consumers in a globalised financial world.

Building awareness about the benefits of AI in remittances is an important step towards increasing adoption. Governments, regulatory organisations and industry participants must properly communicate with users about the increased security, efficiency and personalised services that AI may offer to cross-border financial transactions. Educational efforts can play an important role in providing consumers with the knowledge they need to make educated decisions about using AI-powered remittance services.

Collaboration among stakeholders is critical for promoting a favourable response to AI in remittances. Governments, financial institutions and fintech entrepreneurs should participate in open discussions to develop regulatory settings that promote innovation while protecting consumers. Industry participants may exchange experiences, best practices and work together to build standards that will allow AI technology to be seamlessly integrated into current remittance infrastructures.

Strategic investments in AI infrastructure, talent acquisition and partnerships are critical to accelerating adoption. Financial institutions and remittance service providers should devote resources to developing strong AI capabilities within their organisations. This involves employing competent experts with backgrounds in artificial intelligence, data analytics and cybersecurity. Collaborations with technology businesses may speed up the deployment of AI solutions, providing a competitive advantage in the continuously changing financial sector.

One significant technique for boosting adoption is to promote AI as a tool for financial inclusion. Emphasising how AI may provide financial services to underprivileged groups, particularly in areas with limited access to traditional banking, adds a societal component to the adoption story. Governments and industry actors may collaborate to encourage the use of AI technology to reach the unbanked and underbanked, therefore contributing to overall economic growth.

The implementation of AI in remittances should be considered a strategic investment. Financial institutions that adopt AI technology establish themselves as industry leaders by providing cutting-edge solutions that improve the speed, security and efficiency of cross-border transactions. Demonstrating the practical benefits of AI, such as lower transaction costs and faster processing times, may provide compelling incentives for both enterprises and individuals to adopt these advancements.

Regulatory organisations play an important role in fostering adoption by providing an environment that promotes innovation while assuring appropriate use of AI in remittances. Clear norms and frameworks that handle data privacy, security and ethical concerns give the required guarantees to both enterprises and customers. A legislative framework that combines innovation and consumer safety can boost trust in the use of AI technology.

However, boosting the use of AI in remittances needs a concerted effort that includes collaboration, awareness-raising and strategic investments. AI's revolutionary potential for improving security, efficiency and inclusiveness in cross-border financial transactions makes it a critical driver for the future of remittance services. As stakeholders coordinate their efforts, the application of AI in remittances has the potential to transform the financial environment, providing users with a more smooth and technologically sophisticated experience.

Looking Ahead to the Future of Cross-Border Financial Flows

Anticipating the future of cross-border financial flows offers an engrossing story of innovation and change, with artificial intelligence (AI) integration likely to play a pivotal role. The investigation of cutting-edge technologies, such as blockchain, natural language processing and predictive models, points to a future in which conventional obstacles to cross-border transactions are not only surmounted but also supplanted by a dynamic and linked global financial environment.

One of the key topics in visualising the future of cross-border financial flows is the idea of seamlessness. The use of AI foreshadows a time when transactions would happen automatically and effortlessly, especially when combined with blockchain technology. More than just a theoretical development, the trend towards autonomous financial transactions signifies a real departure from the traditional reliance on middlemen and provides consumers with a more direct and effective way to transact financial business internationally.

Transparency and security are key components that will influence the future environment. Increased security and transparency are a result of the decentralised, tamper-resistant structure of the blockchain and AI's real-time transaction monitoring and analysis. By addressing fraud-related worries and promoting confidence among users engaging in cross-border financial transactions, this paves the way for a more secure global financial ecosystem.

A paradigm shift in the user experience is also anticipated in the future, with a focus on hyper-personalisation and customer-centric services. AI creates highly customised and user-friendly remittance experiences by analysing user behaviour and transaction history. In order to improve happiness and loyalty, users may anticipate personalised advice, expedited procedures and a degree of interaction that goes beyond the bounds of conventional cross-border transactions.

In the future, regulatory compliance—which is frequently a challenging component of cross-border transactions—becomes more proactive and automated. Continuous monitoring for compliance with international legislation, Anti-Money Laundering (AML) requirements and Know Your Customer (KYC) standards is ensured by the integration of AI-driven analytics. In addition to making compliance procedures easier for companies, this establishes the financial sector as a pioneer in the use of cutting-edge approaches to overcome regulatory obstacles.

The evolution of AI to provide market insights and trends portends a more knowledgeable and flexible financial ecosystem, which is expected to shape cross-border financial flows in the future. Businesses may get important insights for strategic decision-making from machine learning algorithms that analyse economic data, market situations and user behaviour. Businesses can traverse shifting market circumstances, adjust to new trends and make well-informed choices in real time with this data-driven strategy.

Blockchain technology and AI have more in common than just improving transaction efficiency. In line with more general developments in decentralised finance (DeFi), it predicts a future in which financial institutions become increasingly automated and decentralised. The shift towards self-governing financial transactions not only simplifies procedures but also fosters a more inclusive and democratic global financial environment where people have more authority over their financial resources and dealings.

Transparency and ethical concerns become essential elements of cross-border financial flows in the future. Foundational principles include protecting user data privacy, reducing biases and using AI systems responsibly. Open dialogue with consumers on the function and implications of AI in remittance services promotes ethical compliance, responsible innovation in the financial industry and trust.

Index

A

GPSR Compliance
The European Union's (EU) General Product Safety Regulation (GPSR) is a set
of rules that requires consumer products to be safe and our obligations to
ensure this.

If you have any concerns about our products, you can contact us on

ProductSafety@springernature.com

In case Publisher is established outside the EU, the EU authorized
representative is:

Springer Nature Customer Service Center GmbH
Europaplatz 3
69115 Heidelberg, Germany